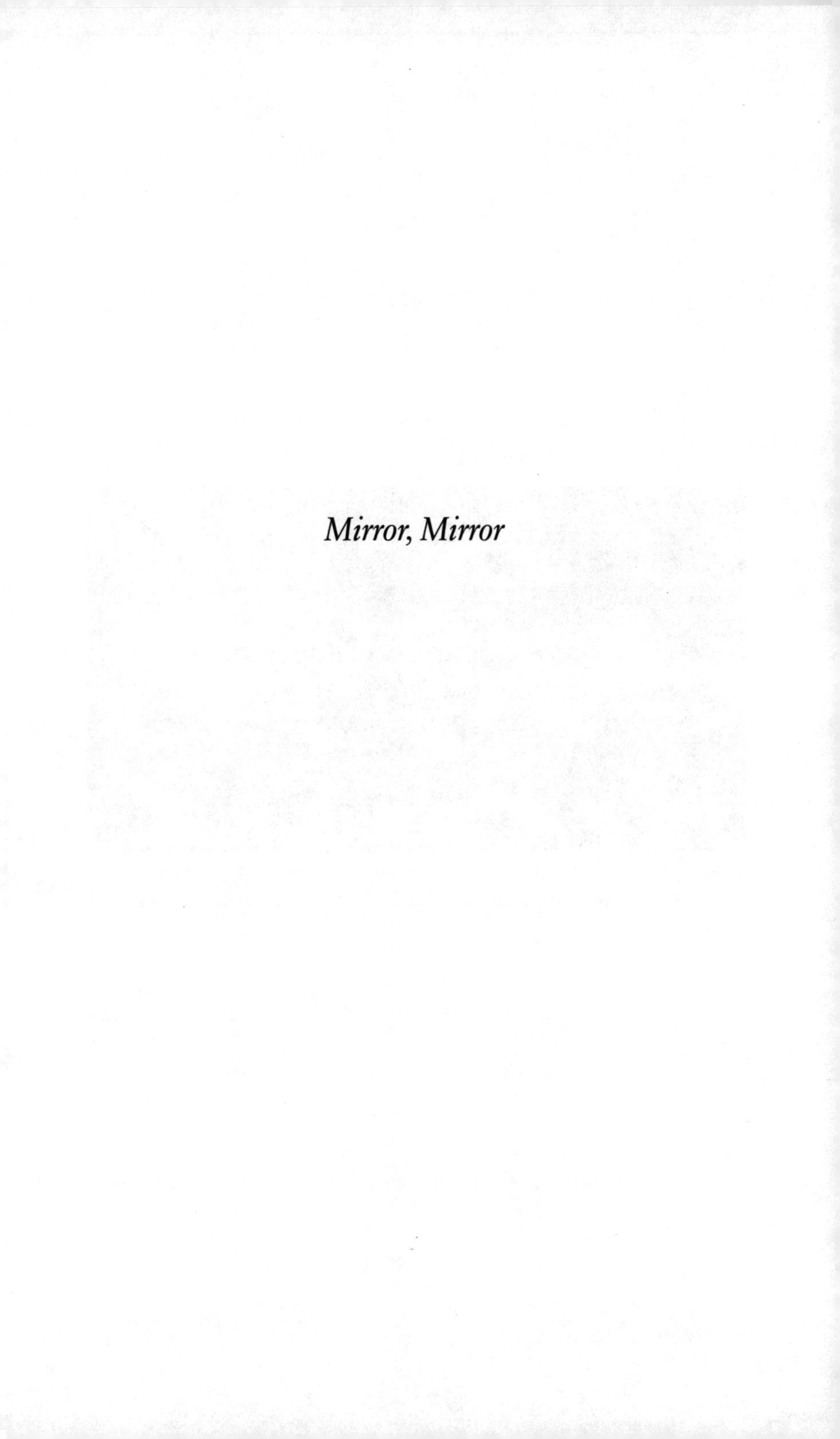

Mirror, Mirror

Francois Lemoyne (Le Moine), 1688–1737, *Narcissus contemplates his image mirrored in water*. Louvre Museum, Paris, France. Photo Credit: Erich Lessing / Art Resource, NY.

Mirror, Mirror

THE USES AND ABUSES OF SELF-LOVE

Simon Blackburn

PRINCETON UNIVERSITY PRESS

Princeton and Oxford

Published by Princeton University Press, 41 William Street, Princeton, New Jersey 08540

In the United Kingdom: Princeton University Press, 6 Oxford Street, Woodstock, Oxfordshire OX20 1TW

press.princeton.edu

Library of Congress Cataloging-in-Publication Data

Blackburn, Simon, 1944–
Mirror, mirror : the uses and abuses of self-love / Simon Blackburn.
pages cm
Includes bibliographical references and index.
ISBN 978-0-691-16142-6 (hardcover)
1. Self-acceptance. 2. Self-esteem. I. Title.
BF575.S37B54 2014
155.2—dc23
2013031309

British Library Cataloging-in-Publication Data is available

This book has been composed in Sabon Next

Printed on acid-free paper.

Printed in the United States of America

10 9 8 7 6 5 4 3 2 1

Sin of self-love possesseth all mine eye
And all my soul and all my every part;
And for this sin there is no remedy,
It is so grounded inward in my heart.
Methinks no face so gracious is as mine,
No shape so true, no truth of such account;
And for myself mine own worth do define,
As I all other in all worths surmount . . .

SHAKESPEARE, SONNET 62

Their vanity was in such good order that they seemed to be quite free of it, and gave themselves no airs; while the praises attending such behavior . . . served to strengthen them in believing they had no faults.

JANE AUSTEN, *MANSFIELD PARK*

Contents

Preface

There are books that should be read like plays: act 1 precedes act 2 and so on to the end. These unfold a plot; they have a story line, and to appreciate the book, this story line has to be faithfully followed. I am not sure this book is like that; while writing it I have sometimes thought it is more like a piece of cake that tastes better when all the layers are chewed together. Perhaps it is more of a perambulation than a quest or a journey. It is, at any rate, an exploration and a meditation. On the other hand, it does have a moral; in fact, two morals. They each concern the complexity of the notions I talk about: pride, vanity, self-esteem, and their cousins. This complexity bedevils the attitudes we should adopt when these traits rear their heads, and confuse any simple moral reactions to them. But they also bedevil empirical work that sets out, sometimes naively, to chart their consequences for good or ill. There is, therefore, a train of thought, but perhaps it is a train in which one can wander at will from one carriage to another.

My principal debt is to the vast cosmetics company L'Oréal and their iconic advertisement: "Because you're worth it." I think of myself as a genial person, so the despair I found welling up whenever I saw this surprised me enough to make me reflect on the themes that are presented here. It is not that I was previously unfamiliar with the vanity of human beings, or even the vanity of human wishes. But there was something particularly blatant about the appeal L'Oréal flaunted that I felt I needed to confront and to understand. It acted like a glimpse into a darker, more wicked world. It is, of course, nothing but the contemporary human world, although I hope not the timeless human world. I give something of my own diagnosis of my reaction in the course of the work.

My second debt is to the context of L'Oréal's appeal: the generation that over the years has so shamelessly implemented the idea that greed is good, that there is no such thing as society, that, because they are worth it, their predations on the common good give them no more than their due. The many bankers, CEOs, remuneration committees, hedge fund managers, tax lawyers, civil servants scuttling through the revolving door into the arms of the great accountancy companies, private medical providers, or arms manufacturers—the many politicians of all stripes with inherited wealth castigating the inadequacies of the poor—all of them so splendidly and shamelessly illustrate the spirit of the age that exaggeration is impossible, parody and satire are silenced (or even co-opted, as we see later), and even anger gives way to blank despair. Doubtless some of us would like to hang these mental and moral deficients from real lampposts, but for the law-abiding among us, verbal ones will have to serve instead.

So, over several years, whenever I had the leisure from more scholarly and perhaps professional pursuits, I found myself jotting down the thoughts that, eventually, I felt able to string together here. I hadn't the confidence to deliver them to the huge variety of fellow workers and audiences that academics like to cite, usually insincerely, as having helped them. In fact, apart from those I have mentioned already, I am only conscious, but extremely so, of the helpful comments of Princeton University Press's readers. I am thankful as well for the support of my agent, Catherine Clarke, and the encouragement and input of Princeton University Press's editor Rob Tempio, copy editor Cathy Slovensky, and, as always, my wife, Angela. I simply hope that there are other readers who echo some of these ideas, and even ones who come to do so.

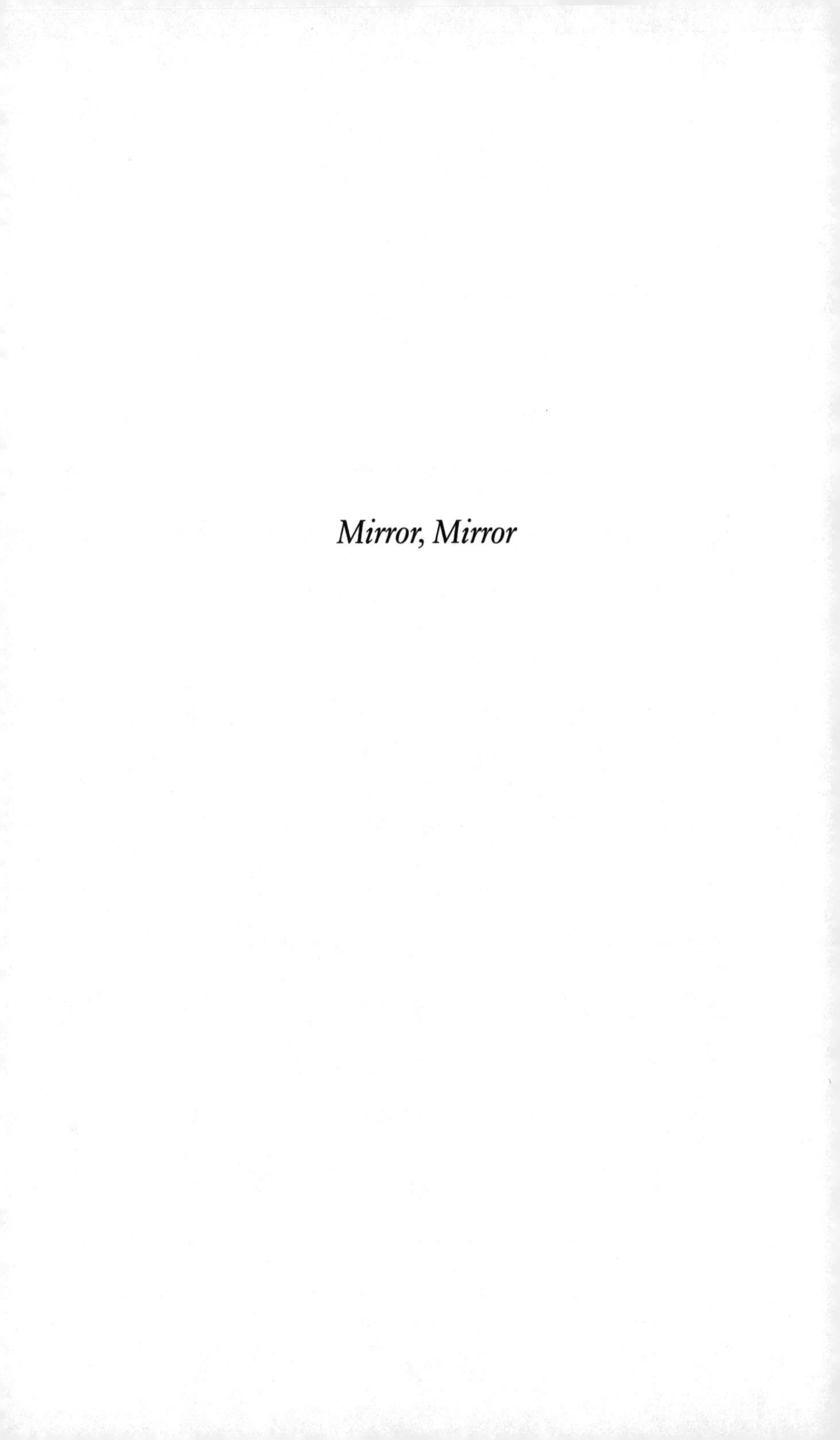

Mirror, Mirror

Introduction

This is first an essay about emotions and attitudes that include some estimate of the self, such as pride, self-esteem, vanity, arrogance, shame, humility, embarrassment, resentment, and indignation. It is also about some qualities that bear on these emotions: our integrity, sincerity, or authenticity. I am concerned with the way these emotions and qualities manifest themselves in human life in general, and in the modern world in particular. The essay is therefore what the great German philosopher Immanuel Kant (1724–1804), never afraid of a grand title, would have called an exercise in pragmatic anthropology:

> Physiological knowledge of the human being concerns the investigation of what *nature* makes of the human being; pragmatic, the investigation of what *he* as a free-acting being makes of himself, or can and should make of himself.[1]

Kant here echoes an older theological tradition that while other animals have their settled natures, human beings are free to make of themselves what they will. So this book is about what we make of ourselves, or can and should make of ourselves.

There is a melancholy pleasure in contemplating the wandering infirmities to which we are all prone. A more strenuous moralist than myself might preach to arm us against them, but I have little such ambition. According to the Scottish philosopher David Hume (1711–76), "the merit of delivering true general precepts in ethics is indeed very small. Whoever recommends any moral virtues, really does no more than is implied in the terms themselves."[2] I pretty much agree. By the time we have grown up, we have learned that courage, justice, kindness, honesty, modesty, open-mindedness, and many other traits are virtues and commendable, and that others such as selfishness, malevolence, laziness, dishonesty, inconstancy, vanity, and pigheadedness are the reverse. When we learn what words others are using about us, we immediately know whether they are praising us or criticizing us. In morality, it is usually not knowledge we lack but the ability to bend our will to it, although there is room for puzzles and dilemmas when morality speaks with two voices. From a rather different angle to Hume's, the Church historian Owen Chadwick, poring over the denunciations of sin in one of the fathers of the monastic tradition, confesses,

> it must be admitted that this expanded catalogue of vice makes for decidedly tedious reading . . . sin, unless it offers hope of scandal, does not interest the human mind.[3]

Enthusiasm for chasing down and denouncing sin is not an attractive human trait. Medieval penitentials (works giving instruction to priests for the handling of confessions) make dull reading, although some are enlivened with delightful stories, rather along the lines of reality TV shows.[4] Even Kant, although he is usually thought of as a strict and rigorous moralist, shies away from undue enthusiasm for virtue, quoting the Roman poet Horace: "The wise man has the name of being a fool, the just man of being iniquitous, if he seeks virtue *beyond what is sufficient*."[5]

Although this is well said, there is another role for critical reflection, or philosophy. People may not need to be taught what counts as wrongdoing and what counts as behaving well. Much knowledge of vice and virtue may well be a fairly democratic possession, learned at one's mother's knee. This, however, is only true of the part of ethics that is concerned with simple and socially enforced rules and prohibitions. It has recently been the principal concern of much modern moral philosophy, which conceives of life in quasi-legal terms as a network of rights and duties derived for the most part from voluntary contracts between individual economic atoms, each with given desires.[6] The danger is that in this picture, a kind of trading becomes the paradigm of moral relations between individuals. This emphasis neglects the domain of self-cultivation, psychological development, or reflection on achieving some kind of harmony or happiness in life that goes beyond satisfaction of whichever desires we happen to have. It also neglects the pervasive influence of culture and context, the "spirit of the age," or the climate of ideas that surround us and play such a large role in directing our thoughts and desires. Yet such reflection used to make up the wider sphere of ethics. Much classical philosophy, not to mention writing on the borderlines where philosophy dissolves into religion, has had precisely this as its topic, with the overt aim of promoting spiritual health, or enabling people to see how to live well. The ancient schools, such as the Cyrenaics, the Cynics, Epicureans, Skeptics, Stoics, and Aristotelians or Peripatetics were largely concerned with offering recipes for this, variously concentrating on self-command, pleasure, friendship, renunciation, citizenship, and virtue, in different mixtures. Similarly, in the religions of the Book, we learn how the true pilgrim, the true trustee of his or her own soul, must pass through the world ignoring most of its blandishments. The pilgrim's progress is not to be impeded by Vanity Fair:

> Therefore at this fair are all such merchandise sold: as houses, lands, trades, places, honours, preferments, titles, countries, kingdoms, lusts, pleasures, and delights of all sorts—as whores, bawds, wives, husbands, children, masters, servants, lives, blood, bodies, souls, silver, gold, pearls, precious stones, and what not.
>
> And moreover, at this fair there is at all times to be seen jugglings, cheats, games, plays, fools, apes, knaves, and rogues, and that of all sorts.[7]

The moral here is that while it is easy to know not to lie to each other, for example, it is a great deal harder to know how to look after our own souls. What we need may even be more self-love, not less, for a truly informed concern for the self may be a very different thing from a blank check to spend at Vanity Fair.

Unfortunately, this kind of exercise can itself descend into banalities: don't overindulge, control yourself, be a good citizen, don't sweat the small stuff, enjoy life, don't ask too much of it, remember how short life is, cultivate friendships, be nice. Philosophers have themselves worried about this: Bertrand Russell, for instance, says of Aristotle's long disquisitions on friendship that "all that is said is sensible, but there is not one word that rises above common sense."[8] So although many people today feel, as others throughout history have felt, that "there must be something more" to life than whatever they are managing to make of it, there is no agreed recipe for discovering what it is.

Perhaps it is the human condition that there cannot be such a recipe, for the idea of an endpoint or goal is illusory. The seventeenth-century writer Thomas Hobbes thought this:

> To which end we are to consider that the felicity of this life consisteth not in the repose of a mind satisfied. For there is no such *finis ultimus* [utmost aim] nor *summum bonum* [greatest good] as is spoken of in the books of the old moral philosophers. Nor can a man any more live whose desires are at an end than he whose senses and imaginations are at a stand.[9]

Restless desire prevents there being any endpoint: like conversation or gardening, living is a process not a product.

Others have supposed that the secret must be to overcome desire altogether. Immanuel Kant came close to claiming this, at least in some moods, regretting that the word "apathy" has fallen into disrepute. Kant's psychology is often portrayed as a kind of Manichean conflict between a pathologically overdeveloped sense of duty, constantly bowing to the categorical imperative, and its great enemy, the seething cauldron of "inclinations," which he seems to have thought of as an almost unmanageable chaos of purely selfish lusts and desires.[10] In this mood Kant chastises ordinary human passions and inclinations as "blind and slavish," and ends up claiming that bliss is the state of "complete independence from inclination and desires." So real self-love would not require gratifying desires but suppressing or destroying them until a final nirvana of total calm descends. To be fair, however, in his later works, and especially in *The Metaphysics of Morals*, it is not complete apathy but only "moral apathy" that he recommends, and this means not that we are to have no feelings but that whatever feelings we have must remain subservient in practice to obedience to the moral law. This is a good deal more palatable, for we all want the desires people have and the inclinations that people feel to be suitably subject to whatever checks decency and morality put upon them.

Rae Langton eloquently illustrates the trouble with ordinary apathy or failure of affect as an ideal in a classic paper, citing the sad example of a particularly enthusiastic follower of Kant.[11] The young girl Maria von Herbert, a correspondent of Kant and an avid disciple of his philosophy, indeed found her life drained of all desire. The reason was that she had lost her one true love, and the reason she had lost him was that she had felt morally obliged to confess a previous indiscretion to him, in conformity to the categorical imperative.[12] But her state was not one of blissful nirvana but of desolation and despair, and it finally ended in her tragic suicide. The categorical imperative acts as a kind of filter or check on whether it is permissible to act on an inclination. But if you have no inclinations, it too has nothing left to do. For most of us, fortunately, life offers many possible sources of satisfaction—science, art, music, poetry, friendship, family, achievement—but any of these might fail to enkindle us, and if we approach them without eros or desire, they will. The result is desolation rather than contentment. This, incidentally, is almost certainly part of the reason why widely prescribed SSRI drugs (selective serotonin reuptake inhibitors) that work to flatten emotion and affect also have apathy, loss of libido, and suicide as significant side effects.[13]

Insofar as Kant had a mistrust of inclination and desire, he was preceded by many religious traditions. The pious resignation of the self into the hands of God can share much with Maria von Herbert's desolation, and religious melancholy is not an uncommon phenomenon. Kant was preceded as well by the Stoics, preaching a life of calm and fortitude, dwelling on the insignificance of our own individual trials in the great cosmic scheme of things. The counsel is to abandon our usual self-centered perspective and endeavor to see the world under the heading of eternity, trying to take ourselves to a purely objective view, God's view, a view from nowhere and nowhen, in which petty human affairs shrink into virtual nothingness. It is to make ourselves into iron men, monsters of fortitude, self-sufficient, independent of the ways of the world or the accidents that happen to us, resolute in the discharge of our duties, yet all the while undisturbed by whatever befalls.

It's very high-minded, and there may even be something sublime about it as an ideal. It is a tough school for heroes and patriots, but it is open to the objection that when life throws its all-too-real problems at us, this kind of wisdom literature is more apt to provoke us than console us. Worse, failing to live up to these ideals, we may ravage ourselves with guilt and misery. We are not iron men. We are buffeted by misfortunes, frequently dependent on other people, far from immune to fears, hopes, griefs, and desires.

It is not in our natures, nor should it be, to maintain a pure and lofty indifference to the world as we find it. And we find it from our own point of view, in which the here and now inevitably looms large. So when things go wrong, we naturally get upset. A person with the right temperament may be soothed in misfortune by the thought that under the sun worse things have happened and will go on happening to better people. Unfortunately, someone with the wrong temperament may be equally embittered by the sister thought that better things have happened and will go on happening to worse people.

In keeping the Stoics at arm's length, we have Hume on our side:

> Away then with all those vain pretences of making ourselves happy within ourselves, of feasting on our own thoughts, of being satisfied with the consciousness of well-doing, and despising all assistance and all supplies from external objects. This is the voice of pride, not of nature.[14]

Hume goes on to remark that the best one can hope for in this direction is to "compose the language and countenance to a philosophical dignity, in order to deceive the ignorant vulgar," and "the heart meanwhile is empty of all enjoyment, and the mind, unsupported by its proper objects, sinks into the deepest sorrow and dejection." The proper objects that are missing are those that give us pleasure, including security, ease, friendships, family, achievements, and so on—the ordinary affairs of life that we are adapted to make into our concerns.

But Hume is too hard on the Stoics, and, surprisingly, not quite on top of human psychology at this point. The Stoics have a more humane side that makes some room for "eupatheia" or good feelings. It is fitting, for instance, to feel grief for the death of a child or a friend. The classical Stoics, including Seneca, Epictetus, and Marcus Aurelius, thus temper the wind to the shorn lamb. They know that we are going to be liable to these emotions, so the recipe becomes not so much to try to be indifferent to things as to maintain decency, composure, or moderation when they threaten to overwhelm us. We are to get a grip on ourselves, take a deep breath, and preserve our dignity through life's inevitable buffets. Examples of the fortitude of others may help, and so sometimes might exercises of reflecting on the size of the cosmos and the insignificance of all human life, including our own.

And contrary to Hume, dignity and decorum are not put on to deceive the ignorant vulgar but are taken up rather like uniforms or routines in the military, so as to provide order and to give shape and boundaries to the emotional lives we are all bound to lead. The ideal is rather that of being the master of one's fate or captain of one's soul.[15] It was sometimes paradoxically expressed by the idea of everything being indifferent, but some things being "preferred indifferents"—a phrase that hardly wears its meaning on its face. The idea, however, is that some things are certainly preferred, or ought to be preferred. But if things don't fall out as we would like, we must exercise self-control. We must know how to cope with the situation and to preserve our ability to carry on. We are to retain our balance; we are not to be capsized. Such an ideal is not trivial; indeed, the phrase "captain of my fate, master of my soul" itself comes at the end of the famous inspirational poem "Invictus" (unconquered) by the Victorian poet W. E. Henley, who wrote it as a teenager, when tuberculosis in the bone meant that he had to suffer having one leg amputated:

> Out of the night that covers me,
> Black as the pit from pole to pole,
> I thank whatever gods may be
> For my unconquerable soul.[16]

For this, the more humane side of Stoicism, it is the stiff upper lip in the face of adversity that is admirable, not the kind of anaesthetized, melancholy indifference that doesn't feel the adversity in the first place. And a determination to remain the master of one's fate is an unalloyed good thing: there are impressive narratives of its success in enabling people to endure horrific circumstances.[17] And it also comes down to the modern world in a form that preoccupies us later, which is the existentialist ideal of taking command, or recognizing our freedom to reject whatever conventional or oppressive scripts society may have written for us to follow.

Retaining self-mastery may require a kind of pride or self-respect, which is one feeling around which this book circles, arguing that it is at the center of a constellation of attitudes to the self, including self-esteem, arrogance, vanity, narcissism, and others. Some of these are regrettable, others essential. Generally they vary, being benign in some forms and not in others: if we reject the ideal of giving up desire and passion altogether, we might still worry about whether there are dispensable desires, idiotic desires, unsatisfiable desires, and, if so, which they are. So it all depends on how emotions bearing on oneself are embedded in one's life. Pride, for example, may be, as Christianity holds, the root of all evil, the chief of the seven deadly sins, or it may instead be something that is absolutely essential to protect, a prime motivator to good behavior, determination, tenacity, and courage, a guarantor of our integrity, a lifeline to which to cling—something, in fact, of which to be proud. Pride, it has been well said, is only tolerable in adversity; by motivating a fight against defeat, it consorts with courage and the preservation of dignity. As we discuss in chapter 7, Satan's pride in Milton's *Paradise Lost* is admirable when it is mostly shown in his courageously staring down the dreadful fate he has brought upon himself. His pride was only bad when it displayed itself as a rejection of all that is good.

Perhaps understanding how to balance these opposing assessments might even assist us to live with ourselves, or at the very least to understand why we might find it difficult to do so. And that in turn might have some use in life's affairs, as Kant hoped, even if two centuries before him, the skeptical Michel de Montaigne had rather charmingly thrown even that into doubt:

> If others examined themselves attentively, as I do, they would find themselves, as I do, full of inanity and nonsense. Get rid of it I cannot without getting rid of myself. We are all steeped in it, one as much as another; but those who are aware of it are a little better off—though I don't know.[18]

I hope Montaigne's final doubt was wrong. The great forerunner of the Enlightenment, Benedict Spinoza (1632–77), also thought that freedom lay in replacing inadequate ideas of things with further understanding, and my belief is that we could all do with a bit more of that. In any case, I think it is terrific fun to explore how we might do so.

1

The Self

Iris Murdoch and Uncle William

Selves are everywhere. I myself and you yourself are but two of them. And they are the focus of much of our attention. We talk of self-abasement, self-awareness, self-belief, self-control, self-denial, self-disgust, self-esteem, and so on through the alphabet, past self-hatred and self-love to self-respect, self-searching, self-trust, and self-violence. My *Oxford English Dictionary* lists eighty-seven such hyphenations before the end of the letter *c*, but after that I lost count. Perhaps there should be more, since with a few exceptions we can have just about any attitude toward ourselves that we have toward other people, or even to things in the world. The exceptions only include such trivial things as my finding you in my way, which is possible, as opposed to finding myself in my way, which is arguably not, except metaphorically when perhaps it is all too possible.

Some moral philosophers give much of this very bad press. In passages such as the following, Iris Murdoch rails against the "self-assertive movements of deluded selfish will," contrasting it with the way that love and truth put us on the right track:

> The love which brings the right answer is an exercise of justice and realism and really *looking*. The difficulty is to keep the attention fixed upon the real situation and to prevent it from returning surreptitiously to the self with consolations of self-pity, resentment, fantasy and despair.[1]

> Humility is a rare virtue and an unfashionable one and one which is often hard to discern. Only rarely does one meet somebody in whom it positively shines, in whom one apprehends with amazement the absence of the anxious avaricious tentacles of the self.[2]

> There is nothing mysterious about the forms of bad art, since they are the recognizable and familiar rat-runs of selfish daydream. Good art shows us how difficult it is to be objective by showing us how differently the world looks to an objective vision. We are presented with a truthful vision of the human condition in a form in which it can be steadily contemplated.[3]

In this view, with attention to the self come delusions, inability to see situations as they are, avarice, fantasy, self-pity, resentment, and despair. Perhaps they do, although perhaps they come in other ways as well, as we shall see in chapter 4. But we can certainly be suspicious of people who cannot be "taken out of themselves," for instance, through devoting attention to others, or even through being carried away by other things, such as great art, music, or spectacles of nature. People who cannot throw themselves into things because of the worm of self-consciousness, typically prominent during adolescence, labor under a serious handicap.

Iris Murdoch's target, however, is far from clear. On the one hand we have the self-conscious adolescent, say, unhealthily preoccupied with the way in which he or she appears to other people. It is not difficult to find that state deplorable, and the cure, alongside simply growing up, may well be to pay more attention to other things. However, the self-conscious adolescent need not be particularly selfish, and selfish people need not be particularly self-conscious: indeed, sublimely selfish people are typically unaware of their elephantine footprints. A fixed disposition to safeguard or improve one's own position, even at the expense of others, does not have to be conscious. It can manifest itself in a lifelong habit of absentmindedly taking lots of anything that ought to be shared more equitably, or backing away when there are unpleasant things to be done, or finding oneself certain that the rest of the family will also enjoy whatever you want to do. *Sesame Street*'s Miss Piggy can say "Selfish? Moi?" with sincere surprise. The businessmen we meet later may think of themselves as merely doing their job, simply servants of their calling.

Iris Murdoch's recipe for avoiding either selfishness or self-consciousness is that we should pay serious attention to other things, which she casually identifies with achieving a kind of objective, God's-eye view of the world and our place in it, and here too there is surely room for doubt. So, commenting on the last of the three passages, the critic John Carey mocks the alleged objectivity of great art:

> Are the paintings of El Greco or Rubens or Turner objective? Or the poetry of Milton or Pope or Blake? Or the fiction of Swift or Dickens or Kafka? . . . Murdoch's proclamation seems the exact reverse of the truth. If we had to choose between objectivity and her term "selfish daydream" as the principle behind art then it would have to be "selfish daydream," though we might want to rephrase it as "individual imaginative vision."[4]

An artist who erases his or her own personality is not going to be an artist at all. Carey is surely right to query the ideal of the innocent or impersonal eye, unencumbered with cultural or personal slants on things. All recent philosophy of perception has stressed the way in which expectations, emotions, moods, or a sense of opportunities and obstacles infuse our perception of the world. Indeed, supposing that we are free of personal elements, just seeing things as God intended them to be seen, or in the only way that it could be right to see them, might itself reasonably be classed as a complacent exercise of the "big fat ego" about which Iris Murdoch seemed so worried.[5]

We may be even more doubtful about the association between selfishness and lack of an objective vision. In 1968 at an auction at Aldwick Court in Somerset, a ring of art dealers conspired not to bid against one another to buy a hitherto unrecognized Madonna and Child by the great Sienese artist Duccio di Buoninsegna. They therefore paid only £2,700 (around $4,000) for it, and scurrying away they promptly sold the painting to the National Gallery for £140,000 (more than $200,000). Their vision seems to have been excellent: they saw the painting exactly for what it was, when other people did not. But their keen perception was also entirely at the service of their greed, and indeed criminally so, although by the time the ring came to light, the date for a possible prosecution had passed. Many a connoisseur will look more acutely at things when he anticipates possessing them. Selfishness motivates, and can sharpen one's attention to crucial detail.

So we have excessive attention to the self, or self-consciousness, and excessive demands on behalf of the self, or selfishness, as things to avoid. But we should also remember that a sense of self is a precious thing. Envisage someone losing it, not knowing who she is. We might think of Iris Murdoch's humble saint who "never thinks of herself," but we might think instead of the terrifying state of those who have lost any sense of their own self, and cannot seize on any self to think of. This might be through advanced Alzheimer's disease or some similar incapacity. Take away someone's memory and you leave them bewildered, lost, living only in the present, surprised, frightened, or even angry at the constantly unfamiliar scenes they remain able to perceive but not to remember or place in sequence. Our identities are the lifelines used to guide our journey: even knowing where we are implies enough of knowing who we are to keep our bearings. Otherwise, experience becomes what Kant called "a mere kaleidoscope of sensations, less even than a dream."[6] King Lear's tragedy is largely one of the terrifying loss of this lifeline, the disintegration of the self. Under the impact of terrible traumas, such as those of disaster and battle, survivors have to struggle to put the fragments back together, to rebuild themselves. Lear is reduced to animal cries, and the victims of severe psychological trauma often cannot speak:

> Like most of the 4th I was numb, in a state of virtual dissociation. There is a condition . . . which we call the two-thousand-year-stare.

> This was the anaesthetized look, the wide, hollow eyes of a man who no longer cares. I wasn't to that state yet, but the numbness was total. I felt almost as if I hadn't actually been in battle.[7]

To recover himself would be to recover his voice, his ability to attend to the world around him, to rejoin the activities and conversations of others.

Philosophers have found it puzzling that the central character in all this drama is surprisingly absent from the stage. David Hume put it like this:

> For my part, when I enter most intimately into what I call myself, I always stumble on some particular perception or other, of heat or cold, light or shade, love or hatred, pain or pleasure. I never can catch myself at any time without a perception, and never can observe any thing but the perception. When my perceptions are removed for any time, as by sound sleep; so long am I insensible of myself, and may truly be said not to exist. And were all my perceptions removed by death, and could I neither think, nor feel, nor see, nor love, nor hate after the dissolution of my body, I should be entirely annihilated, nor do I conceive what is farther requisite to make me a perfect non-entity.[8]

It sounds as though Hume had hoped to find a constantly present "thing," only to find that there is no such constant presence as we go our everyday ways. There is only the ongoing life of the one animal, and the thoughts and desires and intentions that make up that life do not include the self as an element in the scene, in the way that the Albert Hall or Statue of Liberty might be. These have an independent existence: they are there whether or not we notice them or think about them, and there is something new and identifiable in our experience when they literally come into view. But selves seem to be creatures of consciousness. Without self-awareness in its various forms, there is no self left. Yet what is it of which we are aware? Not just the body, because one may be aware of one's body without being aware of it as one's own, as when we see a momentarily unrecognized fat person in a mirror. What then is the "I" behind my eyeballs, the subject inhabiting my brain and body, the being who survives life's changes, that wakes up afresh every morning, and that hurtles or falters forward to its inevitable end?

If Hume is right, the self has disappeared, in which case perhaps we cannot think about ourselves at all. Some versions of both Buddhist and Hindu religions hold this. They both have "anatta" or "no self" traditions that deny the reality of the self, and see this discovery as liberation from chains of self-concern and self-love that otherwise fetter us and weigh us down. It would be nice for moralists if the fact that the self is elusive did have this moral implication, freeing us without effort from Iris Murdoch's tentacles of selfishness. But unfortunately, it does not do so: there is no royal road from anatta to agape, or diffuse, general love of others. The illusion or fiction of a self, if that is what it is, leaves us capable of excesses of self-love or self-interest, just as it leaves us capable of deficiencies of self-knowledge or self-confidence. And in spite of his difficulties over finding a "self" of which he was aware, Hume almost immediately followed his discussion with an analysis of pride, an emotion that is only identifiable in terms of a pleasurable belief in something admirable about oneself. He was too well grounded to think that self-centeredness would wither because of metaphysical puzzles, although other, more hopeful philosophers have argued that whether or not it does, it certainly ought to do so.[9]

The problem is that even if, from the point of view of the universe, your toothache is exactly as bad as my toothache, it is inevitable that the latter matters to me and motivates me in quite a different way from the former. However much compassion I can summon up for you, the one is quite different from the other. I might recognize that from the point of view of the universe, it is just as good if my twin brother goes to Venice as if I do, and if I love him like a brother, I might be just as happy if he does. But it is still different if he goes and not I, and in the ordinary desires and motivations of life, that difference matters. No metaphysics is likely to erase the distinction between "mine" and "thine," although moralists can certainly urge us to soft-pedal it whenever we can.

Yet how can this be so if the self is elusive to the vanishing point? Perhaps the clue to the conundrum lies in those endless hyphenations: the noun "self," with its elusive object, is perhaps an unnecessary if tempting abstraction from all-too-real processes such as self-assertion, selfishness, self-doubt, and the others. Just as we do not need to look around the world for "sakes" in order to make sense of doing something for the sake of someone, so we may not need to look for selves to make sense of the processes that we use the word to describe.[10] We do not need to believe in souls in order to find some people soulful.

Cognitive scientists and philosophers reflecting on their work like to think of the mind as evolving from the interactions between a large number of unintelligent components, just as the working of a computer can derive from a large number of individually dumb transformations of strings of zeroes and ones. The mind is like a club or nation, an aggregate that emerges from the relationships between the elements that make it up. Our minds, or we ourselves, emerge from this swarm of dumb happenings. But there need be no central control room, no inner manager to whom messages are delivered and from whom instructions emerge. There is just the activity of the whole, but nothing constant or unchanging. There is an organized orchestra but no conductor; a government, but nobody sitting on a throne receiving messages and issuing orders. There are processes, but no inner agent guiding and directing them. When the processes happen properly, then we as agents do things and decide things, but we are the upshot of the processes, not the sovereign who controls them. We are the lumbering and all-too-physical animals, not the ghostly controllers upstairs in their attics. An animal needs no such thing; its own control of its own actions lies in the multiple interactions of its neural circuits and chemical messengers.[11]

The elusive self that Hume could not find is sometimes called the self as "metaphysical subject," the "I" who thinks and acts and perceives and rejoices or suffers, and who is thought of as set over and against all the rest of the world. Asked what it is, the Buddha is said to have replied by remaining silent, suggesting that it somehow defies description or analysis. Thinking of the self as a kind of thing is making the subject into an object. It is making it a thing in the world, and I agree with those philosophers who suggest that this is an illusion. It is in this vein that Ludwig Wittgenstein wrote:

> There is no such thing as the subject that thinks or entertains ideas.
>
> If I wrote a book called *The World as I Found It*, I should have to include a report on my body, and should have to say which parts were subordinate to my will, and which were not, etc., this being a method of isolating the subject, or rather of showing that in an important sense there is no subject; for it alone could *not* be mentioned in that book.[12]

The self, in this story, is like the eye that cannot be a given in its own visual field. Its elusive nature can usefully be compared with the elusive nature of the place from which you see things, or the time at which events are happening. Thus, suppose you find yourself in an instant transported to the middle of a desert or ocean. You can see in all directions—but unless you have other clues, what you see does not tell you where you are. Or suppose that like Rip Van Winkle you regain consciousness after a long sleep or coma. You see what is happening around you—but that does not tell you what time it is. Time and place function as points of reference from which things are experienced, but are themselves no part of the experience. Perhaps selves are like that.

Wittgenstein drew an interesting conclusion from this:

> Here it can be seen that solipsism, when its implications are followed out strictly, coincides with pure realism. The self of solipsism shrinks to a point without extension, and there remains the reality coordinated with it.[13]

It is rather wonderful to think that solipsism, the monstrous limit of egoism, the idea that I am the only entity in the cosmos, with everything else being only part of a virtual reality spun out of my own consciousness, coincides with "pure realism," or confidence in the everyday, commonsense, independent world that existed before me and will exist after me. Solipsism seems to be the ultimate limit of skepticism, but rather as extreme communism comes to seem uncannily like extreme fascism, according to Wittgenstein, solipsism evaporates into simple realism. It does so just because the "metaphysical subject" or self of solipsism cannot be given as a "thing" in the world. So the "I" of solipsism diffuses, and all one is left with is the world as one experiences it.

Curiously, however, Wittgenstein himself retained a hankering for reading his equation the other way around, reducing realism to solipsism. One of the more profound, or perhaps annoying, of his gnomic statements is: "so too at death the world does not alter, but comes to an end."[14] This has a highly solipsistic air, for a normal realism about the world would say that it is simply false. When people die, the world goes on, and knowing that this is true might be one of the things we dislike about the prospect of dying, and might even resent about the world. It is so tragically, unbearably *unfair* that there will be other springtimes with flowers and sunshine and birdsong, other festivals, other songs and jokes I shall never hear, panoramas I shall never see, after I am in my grave.[15] If only I had been lucky enough to have been born twenty-five years later, and have a corresponding extension of time to come, it wouldn't be nearly so bad.

A different, although compatible, diagnosis of the elusive nature of the self is found in post-Kantian philosophy, and particularly in existentialism. In this tradition there is no description of the self, or the core or essence of a person's being, because we are always free to cast off or reject any such description (well, let's rein back a bit: you can't reject the description of yourself as, for instance, medium height, English-speaking, overweight, balding, twenty-first-century, middle class, and so on. You are not, and can never be, a Roman centurion, Spanish conquistador, or a native of the Amazonian rain forest with no contact with Western civilization. You cannot shake off the description of yourself as none of those things). Nevertheless, taking a cautious, skeptical, or transgressive stance toward any of the categories that others apply to us is a prime duty of "authenticity," whereas denying one's own ability to do so is the hallmark of an inauthentic, fettered existence tied to the conventional roles into which society has forced us. The authentic person takes control of his or her aims and goals, and thereby takes control of his or her very identity. The undeniable romantic attractions of this ideal occupy us later, as do its considerable difficulties.

Meanwhile, we should reflect that, whatever their elusive nature, selves do not give up easily. Perhaps it would be better to say that thinking in terms of a self that owns experience is a kind of construction of our brains, a mode of organization of the living animal that enables it to cognize other things, although as it does so, its own self remains outside its field of vision. But even that metaphor is misleading, since what lies just outside the field of vision can be brought within it if we turn our heads, while the metaphysical self, apparently, never can be. It is always behind the camera, never in front of it.

Some philosophers have followed up these thoughts by suggesting that the self is a kind of "narrative construct," an illusion of individuality invented in something like the way that a fictional character is invented. The teeming brain somehow turns itself into a novelist, and spins a story about the abiding and permanent self that owns experiences and directs actions. It is as if the advice "pull yourself together" is the advice to write a story rather than the advice to become focused on decision and action. But it is not clear that this view is intelligible, nor that it very accurately maps what most of us are like. The story is doubtfully intelligible, because the storyteller responsible for the fiction is already—what?—surprise, surprise, it is a little self! It has purpose, intentions, command of language—it is just like me, in fact. And it is surely incoherent to suggest that I myself am a fiction in a story that I myself tell—and tell to whom? Why, to me, to myself, of course. I am narrator, audience, and fictional character in the story being told, all rolled into one. Imagination boggles, and rightly, for the story is only fitted to remind us of Tweedledum and Tweedledee's failed attempts to convince Alice that she is but an element in the dream of the sleeping Red King: "'If that there King was to wake,' added Tweedledum, 'you'd go out—bang!—just like a candle.'"[16] "'I know they're talking nonsense,' Alice thought to herself, 'and it's foolish to cry about it.'" Yet even poor Alice wasn't told that if she herself stopped telling her own story, she would go out—bang!—just like a candle. She did, however, begin to worry about that possibility later: "'So I wasn't dreaming after all,' she said to herself, 'unless—unless we're all part of the same dream. Only I do hope it's *my* dream, and not the Red King's! I don't like belonging to another person's dream.'" Part of Carroll's delicious mischief is, of course, that the Alice who says this—the one who has the adventures in the Looking Glass world—is indeed doubly a creature in a dream. She is first a creature in the supposed dream of the real Alice Pleasance Liddell, whom Carroll adored and who lived in Oxford and owned a kitten.[17] But then the plot thickens, for that dream, the dream of the real Alice, was itself not a real dream but only a fictional dream in the story written by Carroll. Fortunately, I, writing this, am not a creature in my own dream nor those of anyone else, and neither are you, reading it.

The idea of the self as a fictional or literary construct has other problems. For many of us, a "novel" about our lives, told, for instance, in order to chart a coherent character visible throughout our somewhat chaotic recollections and contradictory aims, is hardly an imperative. The lying Josiah Bounderby in Dickens's *Hard Times* tried to pass himself off as the hero of a particular kind of narrative, telling exaggerated stories about the hardships of his childhood and the extraordinary courage and perseverance that enabled him to overcome them. But most of us do not need to do this.[18] We can be happy with life being just one thing after another. The Greeks pictured "psyche" as the embodiment of the human soul, as a butterfly, a creature of beauty, but also one of inconstant flutterings, flits, and bobs, and that is at least as apt a model as anything enduring that persists through the changing scenes of life.

It is time to leave these deep waters and pursue more ordinary themes. A better clue to the nature of self-consciousness may be given by everyday examples of people in whom it seems pleasantly absent. We have already touched on Iris Murdoch's saint, but here is an engaging example in which Gwen Raverat, Charles Darwin's granddaughter, writes of his sons, her uncles:

> They were the most unself-conscious people that ever lived, those five uncles; but Uncle William was the most unself-conscious of them all. He hardly knew that he had a self at all. There is a story about him at my grandfather's funeral at Westminster Abbey. He was sitting in the front seat as eldest son and chief mourner, and he felt a draught on his already bald head; so he put his black gloves to balance on the top of his skull, and sat like that through the service with the eyes of the nation upon him.[19]

Gwen Raverat is right that the word "unself-conscious" seems apt to describe this. But paradoxically, as the rest of her narrative makes clear, Uncle William and the other Darwin children seem to have been relentlessly hypochondriac, which implies an overdeveloped concern for one's own state of health, a kind of self-consciousness that can readily consort with selfishness: a species of egoism. And Uncle William's indecorous conduct might also come closer to implying a more serious defect: Is there not something a little bit *shameless* about him? If he really has no consciousness of how he stands in the eyes of others at the very moment of taking such an important part in this grave and dignified ceremony—was he not embarrassed faced with the no doubt pained expressions of the officiating clergy?—then while it may be unworldly and lovable, would it be so good if, for instance, he had decided to take off his itching trousers or accompany the majestic organ by playing on a kazoo?

In other words, taking no notice of the eyes and thoughts of others could be the hallmark of the abandoned villain as much as the lovable uncle. Might not an unself-conscious person monopolize the conversation, unconscious of how he is boring others to death, or for that matter, unself-consciously run away on the battlefield, or unblushingly pocket a dropped purse? Hume said that the minds of men are mirrors to one another, and this mirroring is the constant check we have on our own behavior. Internalizing the actual or potential gaze of others is an essential component of decency. In case this all sounds a little priggish, Hume gives a splendid example:

> A man will be mortified, if you tell him he has a stinking breath; though it is evidently no annoyance to himself. Our fancy easily changes its situation; and either surveying ourselves as we appear to others, or considering others as they feel themselves, we enter, by that means, into sentiments, which no way belong to us, and in which nothing but sympathy is able to interest us.[20]

Of course, the suggestion that one of the intensely upright, Victorian children of such a well-regulated house as that of Charles Darwin might be less than perfectly moral, let alone indifferent to the disgust his bad breath might provoke in others, is outrageous. But we might wonder whether it is good training and long habit that keeps him on the straight and narrow rather than an ability to integrate himself with the perspective of others.

Cicero, the Roman politician and writer, thought that decorum was an important part of virtue, and worries about Uncle William give us a clue into ways that perhaps he was right. Good manners are a small but constant adjustment to the reasonable expectations or needs of others, little tokens acknowledging their right to a certain space, the offering of a certain security in what they may expect from one. They are at the very least a training school for more celebrated virtues like honesty and justice. They are not to be despised, although they can engender their own anxieties and problems. One of the confusing moral lessons children have to learn is to adjust the quite frequent collisions between honesty, which they are taught as absolute, demanding, and inflexible, and the small hypocrisies of decency. The honest child who truly tells his doting grandparents, aunts, or uncles that their birthday present is rubbish in his eyes gets a smart rebuke, and his howling protestations of honesty are dismissed by the outraged and embarrassed parents. *That* kind of honesty is not required, or even tolerated. Social life requires a good amount of acting. Courtesy trumps honesty, which must give way to deference to the feelings of others. We disguise this from ourselves, saying that we must tell the truth, the whole truth, and nothing but the truth, yet voicing every belief that flits into our minds is catastrophically far from the way to win friends or keep them.[21]

So however things stood with Uncle William, the rest of us can certainly monitor ourselves, sometimes obsessively, as all those hyphenated terms in the dictionary reminded us at the outset. But it is not quite like thinking of other things. Uncle William's charming deficit suggests that our sense of self is intimately tied to our sense of our place in the eyes of others, or, in other words, in the moral or social world. Contrary to the existentialists, we might sympathize with the idea that *what* we are is fully exhausted by *who* we are: husband, father, citizen, teacher, soldier . . . . The Oxford philosopher R. G. Collingwood put it admirably:

> The child's discovery of itself as a person is also its discovery of itself as a member of a world of persons. . . . The discovery of myself as a person is the discovery that I can speak, and am thus a persona or speaker; in speaking I am both speaker and hearer; and since the discovery of myself as a person is also the discovery of other persons around me, it is the discovery of speakers and hearers other than myself.[22]

The power of this idea to compromise the rival ideal of authenticity occupies us later. Meanwhile, it suggests that our sense of self is reciprocal with our sense of other people, and their sense of us. We discover ourselves only in the social world. Hence, moral notions enter into the most important dimensions of self-consciousness, and our sense of self is largely made up by them. They compose our identity.

Although this goes some way to undermining the idea of untrammeled freedom, Collingwood's insight is in fact echoed in Sartre's account of recognizing another person as being a *subject*, as having a point of view. Within that other person's point of view, one is oneself as much an *object* as he or she may be for oneself. Being an object for another person includes being subject to his or her evaluations. Hence, recognizing another subject is potentially a destabilizing experience: the recognition that the sovereignty that it is natural to claim for oneself is no better founded than that which other people are also going to claim for themselves. It also involves the possibility of being ashamed, as falling short in the eyes of others, of needing to hide oneself. In one of Sartre's celebrated vignettes, a man is sneaking a look through a keyhole at some interesting scene within. He is wholly absorbed, and his own self is absent from his view and from his thoughts. But a creaking floorboard behind him changes everything. He is now conscious of himself as appearing to another, and, of course, as not appearing to best advantage, in fact, to being revealed as a Peeping Tom. With interpersonal consciousness comes the awareness of evaluative perspectives within which one is not automatically on a pedestal, but on the contrary always at danger of being an object of judgment or even of derision or contempt.

A very nice psychological observation shows the power of this idea. In Newcastle University Psychology Department, there was a communal coffee room in which there was an honesty box, with an ordinary piece of A4 paper (about 21 by 29 centimeters or 8 by 11 inches) indicating the modest schedule of payments people were expected to make for their tea, coffee, milk, and so forth. Unfortunately, it appeared that not nearly enough money was being placed in the box: psychologists are just as good as everyone else at freeloading. The member of the department in charge of the system, Melissa Bateson, decided to vary the notice by indicating the sums due, not by adding capital letters or threats, but just by varying a little banner illustration along the top of the notice. On some weeks it would be a neutral frieze of flowers. On other weeks the picture showed the eyes of a face looking directly at the viewer.

The notice was not particularly conspicuous, but on weeks with the eyes looking at them, people stumped up nearly three times as much as on weeks without them. The mere possibility or mere idea of being seen to be defecting from a social duty was enough to change behavior dramatically. Similar results have been found with students who are given an opportunity to cheat on a test. "Primed" by being told casually that the room in which they sit is thought to have a ghost, fewer people cheat than if there is no such priming. Even an invisible agency looking at you is enough to motivate you back onto the straight and narrow. This is presumably one of the adaptive functions of religions that often emphasize God's all-seeing eye.

Of course, if one is sufficiently shameless, brazen, brass-necked, unimaginative, insolent, or in the limit psychopathic, there is no internalization of the point of view of others. Their view of you has no authority for you. We return to this sinister list later when discussing the insidious mechanisms we have for discounting the actual or potential gaze of others.

Returning to identity, what really makes you the individual you are is given in your unique history, the stream of experiences belonging to you and nobody else, surveyable by you in memory but crucially extensible by you through your choices, decisions, and aims for the future. You are someone with a country, family, history, particular social life, set of projects, and set of boundaries within which there are things you will do, and beyond which lie things you will not do. You have habits of behavior, and you have claims on others and expectations of them, just as they have in regard to you. All these things make up your social and moral world. Your identity, in fact.

The word "moral" may sound rather serious here, and it is natural to be suspicious of too much talk about it. But we need not mean anything unduly high-minded. Consider a normal day, not one on which you are bent on saving the world or rectifying its injustices. You get up, perhaps because you must, since your job or family requires it. You compliment one child on his homework and sympathize with another for some setback. You are grateful to your spouse for thoughtfully showing you where you left your keys. On the journey to work, you suffer a flash of anger as someone disrespectfully barges past you, but you suppress the desire to retaliate. You are plunged into despair because a colleague whose work is inferior to yours has been given a promotion over you, and you vent your resentment at lunchtime, taking consolation from the sympathy of your audience.

And so on and so on, in an endless dance of social interactions, mediated by emotions of sympathy or resentment, thoughts of what is proper, what is annoying, what is a grievance, what you deserved, what others deserved, what needed doing, what was acceptable, and what was or would have been out of line. Meanwhile, in your head you rehearse the sayings and doings, real or imagined, of friends, family, politicians, or people you have heard of. This pattern of reactions to such events and such thoughts make up your day, and every day (we could go on: James Joyce's *Ulysses* gave 265,000 words to an ordinary day in the life of Leopold Bloom, an ordinary man, whose memories and daydreams flit and bob along in their butterfly-like way). The pattern in turn gives other people their sense of who you are—your character or personality—your very self. And you are self-conscious as the owner of thoughts, even if the thoughts are not about yourself.

Even after we abolish the idea of a metaphysical subject, we can after all describe ourselves by finding ourselves in our world. We do so in James Joyce's way. After six hundred pages or so, we know Leopold Bloom—and we know him as well as he knows himself. Joyce did not find something different from the living man—something inside him, as it were, that pulled the strings or determined the course his thoughts took. He just described his life, which included the things he found himself doing, and the thoughts that came, unbidden, into his head. These are processes, things that happen, one damn thing after another. There was nothing else to describe, and it is these processes that we remember and reflect upon when we think about who we are.

So I can after all loom large in my own thoughts. I may dwell on my own past doings, with shame or pleasure. I can dwell on my own prospects, with hope or fear. If I do this too much, then I am self-obsessed and may be self-destructive. If I do it too little, then I may be charming, unworldly, and spontaneous like Uncle William (let's give him the benefit of the doubt), or perhaps thoughtless and careless, if, myself having too little self-concern or self-awareness, I am also unconcerned and careless about others around me.

I can be more or less sympathetic with the similar hopes and fears, shames and pleasures of other people, although never quite in the same way. For after all, if it was I who did that embarrassing thing, the memory makes me blush, whereas if it was you who did it, the memory may be more likely to make me laugh (although we can also blush with embarrassment at the shame—or even at the lack of shame—of another person). If it is I who am to undergo a serious operation, I feel different from if it is you, however much my compassion may bridge the divide. And this is partly because I may have to decide things if it is me, whereas if it is you, then it is up to you. We cannot make others' decisions for them.

Hence, selves have a perfectly good place in our thoughts. Just as there is a difference between my friend Fred going to Machu Picchu and my friend George going there, so there is a difference between I myself going there and either of them doing so. I am a person among others, so how can there be any error in my taking account of that fact in my thoughts and desires?

Of course, sadly, the elderly man who gets to Machu Picchu may not be much like the sprightly youth who anticipated going there. His connection with the sprightly youth may not be through any identity of interests, hopes, intentions, abilities, or habits. His memories will be very different, and who knows how his personality may have been altered by time? There may only be a thread of biological, animal continuity, a long process of cellular division, change, and death, connecting him with the earlier youth. Perhaps he is going not because of the excited anticipation that animated the youth but from a kind of weary loyalty to a plan he dimly remembers forming long ago. The times change, and we change with them, and it is futile to look for a self that does not change while all its properties and relationships do so. "My self" is better thought of as "my life," a process that is extended in time and embracing the whole sequence of static instants from birth to death. And the most important things about this process are the relations it has to the social environment: the circle of those others whose takes on me so infuse my take on myself.

Sonnet 62, quoted at the beginning of this book, continues with a complex reversal of the flamboyant admission of self-love:

> But when my glass shows me myself indeed
> Beated and chapped with tanned antiquity,
> Mine own self-love quite contrary I read;
> Self so self-loving were iniquity.
> 'Tis thee, myself, that for my self I praise,
> Painting my age with beauty of thy days.

The author looks in the mirror, which gives the lie to his vanity. He recovers, in a manner, in the final two lines, addressing his beloved as a "second self," an integral part of his own self, and borrowing reason to be happy with himself from the beauty of his beloved. The general moral we can draw is that by drawing other people or other things into our lives, we can gain more reason for self-contentment, or even self-love, than mere "introspection" can ever provide.

Iris Murdoch was writing in a venerable, philosophical vein when she bemoaned the intrusive self. Whether it is the Christian abomination of pride as the root of all evil, or the Stoic preaching of self-mastery, or the preceding Buddhist teaching that we should study to transcend ourselves, all seem agreed that many of the hyphenated states we mentioned at the beginning are a Bad Thing, and that to become truly wise or happy or content, we must learn to liberate ourselves from the shackles of the self. Uncle William should after all be our model. Perhaps it is time to look further at why we might think that this is so.

2

Liriope's Son

His name will occur on subsequent pages, so we should start by knowing his history. According to the Roman poet Ovid, when he was born, his mother, Liriope, a water nymph, had asked the blind seer Tiresias whether her son would live to enjoy a ripe old age.[1] Tiresias said he would, "if he shall himself not know." This bizarre prediction from the highly reliable Tiresias contradicted one of the most important pieces of advice of the classical world. "Know thyself" was the inscription famously written on the entrance to Apollo's oracle at Delphi, the most important shrine in ancient Greece. The Greeks well understood that lack of self-knowledge is one of the mainsprings of human stupidity and folly. How then could ignorance of himself be the key to a long and happy life for her son, Narcissus?

By the time of the drama that answers this question, the son was some sixteen years old, a shepherd boy, and very beautiful. He had aroused sexual desire and received advances from a great many people, but "hard pride ruled in that delicate frame, and never a youth and never a girl could touch his haughty heart." The nymph Echo was especially aflame with love for him. She had previously suffered the misfortune of annoying the goddess Juno with her chatter, so (perhaps like many of today's twitterati) she had been condemned only ever to repeat the last thing said to her. When Narcissus said "Anyone here?" Echo answered, "Here." When Narcissus said, "Come this way," Echo gladly answered, "This way." Echo threw herself at Narcissus, but he rejected her like all the others. She thereupon wasted away, eventually becoming nothing but the haunting voice we can all hear in the rocks and the woods.

Inevitably, this disdainful young man got his comeuppance, or, as the Greeks phrased it, nemesis awaited him. One day, hot and thirsty from hunting, Narcissus lay down to drink at a quiet pool in the woods where nobody ever came. Here, for the first time, he saw his own reflection:

> And while he slaked his thirst, another thirst
> Grew; as he drank he saw before his eyes
> A form, a face, and loved with leaping heart
> A hope unreal, and thought the shape was real

He became entranced and besotted, and fell in love for the first time in his life: "himself he longs for, longs unwittingly, praising is praised, desiring is desired." But when he reached down to caress the beautiful youth in the pool, the object of his love broke away, as reflections do. He could look and sigh and pine, but he could not touch.

As Ovid tells the story, Narcissus eventually realized that it was he himself he loved, through the medium of his reflection:

> Oh I am he! Oh now I know for sure
> The image is my own; it's for myself
> I burn with love; I fan the flames I feel.
> What now? Woo or be wooed? Why woo at all?
> Would I might leave my body! I could wish
> (Strange lover's wish!) my love were not so near!

But it was too late, and loving himself to the last, he wasted away, like Echo. When others came to bury him, however, there was no body to be found, but only the white and gold flower that we now know as the narcissus. Tiresias had been right after all.

How are we to react to this charming yet more than slightly sinister myth? A superficial view would be that it tells us nothing about ourselves but is simply a story describing a particularly self-obsessed and socially defective young man. A better view—the view of Freud, for example—is that like other myths it can tell us a great deal about ourselves.[2] For example, Narcissus imagines Echo's sayings to be those of a different person, whereas in reality it is only his own voice that is being thrown back at him. So the myth might tell us that the voices we hear in our heads are often not those of other people but our own, falsely imagined to be those of others. The echo chambers of our minds tell us no more than how we appear to ourselves, or imagine ourselves to appear to others. And which of us does not at times dream of the pleasant thoughts others may entertain about us, and the songs of praise that they might, and certainly should, be singing about us? We can easily frame the right words for anyone inclined to admire us. On the other hand, it is extremely difficult and quite painful—two connected obstacles—to dwell on the faults, flaws, or mere foibles we have, and that might, realistically, loom quite large in the conversations of others.

Narcissus might remind us of the swarms of egoists who infest places of interest, art galleries, concerts, public spaces, and cyberspace. For such people, the object of each moment is first to record oneself as having been there and second to broadcast the result to as much of the rest of the world as possible. The smartphone is the curse of public space as people click away with the lens pointed mainly at themselves and only secondarily at what is around them. The egoist imagines all his or her friends fascinated by what they had for breakfast or how they looked standing in front of, or half-obscuring, the *Mona Lisa* or the Taj Mahal. It may be that this is only the contemporary manifestation of the same trait that prompted people to carve their names on monuments and buildings, supposing that for future witnesses, the most interesting thing about the Parthenon or the Venus de Milo would be that John Doe was there. However, the modern world affords opportunities for people to outdo their predecessors. A nice contemporary flowering, or emblem for our times, is the grotesque story of the "Bling Ring," a gaggle of California teenagers whose anxiety to project themselves as celebrities led to them using Google Street View and other modern media facilities to break into the houses of noted celebrities, where they stole expensive trash to imitate the celebrities' lifestyles. They then witlessly incriminated themselves by posting the results to all their social media.[3]

Narcissus did not, however, use the social medium of his day, namely, talking to someone else. He rejected the real nymph, who had a separate voice. He turned her into his own voice in his own head. But our own voice in our own head is not enough for us. However self-satisfied we may be, we need more. We actually need the real voice of others, or perhaps their touch; we are not self-sufficient and indifferent to the world and its other voices. But the egoist and Narcissus coincide in giving themselves instead the imagined voice of others, an ever-present and often reassuring substitute.

The myth also tells us of the delusions attached to desire. What Narcissus desires is unbearably close yet totally unobtainable. The obstacle is not even a solid barrier, yet it is equally impenetrable. And like Narcissus, any of us might die after a life spent chasing phantoms, objects that we cannot possess, and that, if we could but possess them, would turn out to have been nothing but ripples in our minds, illusions and dreams.

Narcissus eventually achieves a genuine self-knowledge, realizing that it is only himself with whom he is besotted. But he cannot use that self-knowledge; he cannot tear himself away from the prism that shows him not the world but only an insubstantial version of his own self. His obsession is incurable. The object of Narcissus's love was only ever going to be himself, even when it was imagined as another. He is the only figure in the drama of his own life, and this kills him. Or rather, it simply deadens his soul; for, after all, at the end there is no body to be found. This strange feature of the myth may suggest that perhaps Narcissus is very much among us, a dead man walking. What the narcissistic self needs is a rebirth, which in a sense Narcissus was given, continuing, however, only as a humble flower whose head is always bowed toward the ground. Or perhaps the absence of a body symbolizes the completeness in the death of the narcissist—his failure to leave any achievement, any memory, or even any mourners. The world goes on as if he had never been. And that in turn might be a lesson that some of the more strident contemporary defenders of the culture of greed and self-absorption would do well to reflect upon.

The object of Narcissus's love behaved ideally in some ways. It was always close, never withdrawing from him more than he himself withdrew from the surface of the pool. When Narcissus reached toward it, it reached forward with exactly the same eagerness and exactly the same intent. It completely reflected his emotions of passion, desire, or grief, just as he felt them. In all these respects it was the perfect object of love—the partner we might all fantasize about, especially when we resent the uncomfortable dissonances provided by other real people. But touch is a more immediate sign of the presence of something real than either hearing or vision, and Narcissus is denied this final gratification. His need and desire are forever unfulfilled.

Narcissus, of course, is besotted by his own beauty. But one might be besotted by something else about oneself: one's own achievements, one's birth, one's possessions, or simply one's own *worth*, or deserved standing in the eyes of the world. These introduce more complex issues that occupy us later, since they bring in the eyes of other people. Vanity, for instance, is most commonly a greedy desire for the admiration and envy of others, and it is not given in the myth that this was any part of Narcissus's problem (we distinguish a rather different form of vanity in chapter 3).

In Ovid's poem there are other examples in which impetuous desire is denied its end because it is fueled only by love of the self. When the god of light and poetry, Apollo, by whom "things future, past and present are revealed," falls in love with the nymph Daphne, he tries to entice her by singing his own praises: "ask who it is who loves you," he pleads, before reeling off his divine credentials.

Daphne, of course, flees from him, deaf to these enticements. As Apollo chases her down, she prays to her father, the river god Peneus, to turn her into a tree, which he does. Apollo, however, is remarkably calm in the face of this obstacle (which, to be fair, he must have seen coming, if his own account of his prophetic powers is to be believed). He simply tells poor Daphne, now a laurel tree, that she can be his very own tree, whose wreath will be a perpetual commemoration of success and fame:

> "My brow is ever young, my locks unshorn;
> So keep your leaves' proud glory ever green."
> Thus spoke the God; the laurel in assent
> Inclined her new-made branches and bent down,
> Or seemed to bend, her head, her leafy crown.

Thinking that the very trees obey you must be a fair candidate for an excess of self-absorption. Apollo's desire is denied its bodily goal, but this leaves his self-image intact, suggesting that Apollo, the god of light, learning, music, and poetry, is after all not so far from Narcissus. For the laurel that Daphne turns into was the universal symbol of success and fame in the classical world. Was the great god Apollo as much ambitious for the applause and admiration of others as for the prize he seemed to have set himself?

Many subsequent poets, including Dante and Petrarch, have meditated on this myth and the dangerous way in which love of fame is just the kind of fault to which poets are especially prone. The poet is supposed to aim for perfection in his art (Daphne when she is herself). But too often he is willing to settle for mere applause from others (Daphne transformed into the laurel crown, the Olympic gold medal). Perhaps indeed he *must* settle for that. There may be magnificent exceptions, but for most practitioners of the arts, self-confidence is a fragile business, utterly dependent on the admiration and support of others. If you can achieve independence from this, well and good, but unless you are a rare genius, and perhaps even then, it will only be by an apprenticeship of reliance on it. The eighteenth-century moral philosopher Adam Smith reflects on the difference between those "noble and beautiful arts, in which the degree of excellence can be determined only by a certain nicety of taste" and those where success admits of "clear demonstration," and insightfully describes how the practitioners of the first will be much more concerned with actual praise, whereas those of the second can rest content with their own certainty of their own successes. He cites distinguished mathematicians "who never seemed to feel even the slightest uneasiness from the neglect with which the ignorance of the public received some of their most valuable works," and goes on to reflect that by contrast authors and poets squabble over praise, form literary factions, and belittle each other with mortal enmity.[4]

There is an enjoyable paradox here. Self-sufficiency requires confidence, and confidence can only be nurtured by the approbation of others. But the paradox is only superficial. It may indeed be true that strength of character needs to be developed by taking on the evaluation of others, but once developed, it has a life of its own. In the same way, honesty and justice in a character may only be developed by means of threats and rewards, but once developed, they render the best people firm in their principles, immune to threats and rewards. So it is that people can be enabled, by the herd, to stand out against the herd.

In principle, therefore, we have the choice of questioning and rejecting even firm and established social norms, and the tendency to do so is a more or less permanent subtext in history, arising whenever there is an open space to see the demands of convention as oppressive, legalistic, restricting, or arbitrary. One kind of reformer is the strenuous advocate of more stringent, less lax, altogether higher standards. Another is the equally common advocate of lower, less demanding, more tolerant standards, and interestingly enough, in one form (antinomianism), this is encouraged by the idea, so convenient to all churches, that faith is all that matters: *sola fide*. If that is so, then it is natural to conclude that as long as we have faith, our behavior makes no difference to the chance of us being saved, in which case we might as well kick over the traces. There may be a permanent tendency for religiously sustained codes to generate just this opposition. Historically, antinomian movements in the West arose when tangles over free will, fate, and God's foreknowledge led to the similar Calvinist idea that we are predestined to heaven or hell and that nothing we can do alters this fate. It is easy to understand how this led various sects to opt for the joyful indulgence of free love, communism, nudism, and other happy aberrations.

Narcissus was in love with himself—or was he? He was in love with a reflection, just as the voices he heard in his head were only his own thoughts or sayings thrown back at him. His reflection was an insubstantial, rippling, changeable thing. It had no anchorage except Narcissus's own face and eyes, which in any case, he could not see. It disappeared as he approached it. Surely our own selves are more substantial than that, perhaps even more fit to serve as objects of devotion than a mere image in the water? There are plenty of voices telling us that this is so, and we meet a contemporary one in chapter 3.

3

Worth It?

The cosmetics company L'Oréal's brilliantly successful marketing slogan "Because you're worth it" has applied equally carefully selected images. In many of them models smile and simper and entice us, projecting the vacant euphoria supposedly attendant on using this or that variety of hair or facial products. However, if occasionally they looked pleasantly human, at least as often they seem to project self-absorption, or arrogance and disdain. They bestow the kind of smile that might as easily be a sneer. They pout and sulk. Their vanity and indifference goes with being above us all, and perhaps with knowing that they can call up our adulation and worship at will. The personae in the advertisements are simply out of our reach. They do not care what we think of them. Like Narcissus, they appear to live in a world of their own, enclosed in their own self-love.

Unsurprisingly, the models calculated to inflame our desires lure us with youth and beauty, and it is relatively easy to see that those are desirable features. We envy those who are handsome or beautiful, graceful, well-proportioned, symmetrical, glowing with youth and health. People mourn the passing of their youth and the fading of their beauty, if they possessed any. Although, when the mirror no longer gives us any pleasure, it is at least worth asking whether this is a loss or a liberation—a freedom from the voice of admiration that we took to be the voice of others, just as Narcissus took the voice of Echo to be. It is much easier for beautiful people to hear in their minds the voice of the world admiring their beauty than it is to hear the envy or malice that will just as probably characterize the real voices outside.

Nevertheless, we can fairly easily understand why youth and beauty are used to lure desire. But why the sulks, or the evident disdain for the rest of the world? Narcissus was, after all, a ridiculous and doomed figure, used to symbolize the ridiculous and doomed nature of self-love. So why are his characteristics those that radiate from the catwalk and the advertisements? In asking this question, I do not deny that sometimes advertisers try for a different image: the alluring smile of the seductress or gigolo, or an empty, zombielike face devoid of emotion or affect altogether, the blank slate on which their customer can inscribe his or her own imaginings. But the disdain is commonly there, and even blankness is a kind of disdain—a refusal of human reciprocity. And the trope is not new: we find it in the eighteenth century, and many other periods. So why is hauteur ever appealing?

In real life it is far from being so. Kant nicely defined arrogance as "an unjustified demand that others think little of themselves in comparison with us, a foolishness that acts contrary to its own end."

The idea is that whenever one issues that demand, or even shows the slightest indication of it, others immediately respond by thinking less of you. Arrogance is one of the least appealing of human traits. Vanity itself has to learn to do without it, as my opening epigram from *Mansfield Park* shows. So, again, why is this horrible character flaw so frequently set up as itself a kind of allurement?

Perhaps we have not fully understood the myth. The strange attraction of these images suggests that our ideals are more complex than we realize. The model, like a Hollywood star, is on a pedestal in our eyes, partly because she is on a pedestal in her own eyes (from now on in this chapter, I shall talk as if a female is both the lure and the target of such advertising. But of course, men can be as well. Indeed, young men in underwear advertisements, for instance, nearly always project an especially loathsome narcissism. We discuss later Rousseau's view of the asymmetry between men and women in respect of vanity). We accept her at her own valuation, which is huge, so huge that she has no need of us, any more than a deity has need of his worshippers. She no doubt manages an icy inward smile with pleasure of being who she is, just as Narcissus might have smiled in his self-induced trance. But she need not smile at us—indeed, to promote this kind of illusion, she must not smile at us—because that would be a gesture of recognition and reciprocity, and the fantasy she is inducing is one in which there is no commerce with people like ourselves. By buying the product, the promise whispers, we can transcend our everyday dependencies on one another and rise to join the royalty and the gods, a higher place where we too can afford to ignore the herds below.

And why would you want to do that? Because you're worth it. In our sober moments we surely doubt ourselves enough not to be sure whether we are worth it. But wouldn't it be nice to be up there on that pedestal, rich enough in our own beauty and self-confidence not to need or care for reciprocity with people as low as we are at present? Of course it would be more than nice, it would be *enviable*—and it wouldn't be unfair either. We might feel lucky if we floated up to the pedestal, but we would not feel that there had been any cosmic injustice about it. It would be no more than we deserve. Because we're worth it.

The hauteur of the persona protects her from the need of compromises and servilities, the need to be nice to others, or to depend on their good opinion. It is not even as if she would pity us for being inferior. It is rather that she could not comprehend the idea of being flawed, dependent, and insecure like us. It simply could not occur to her to pity us for our multiple inadequacies, because we lie outside the range of her imagination (we also meet this later, discussing Rousseau). And look, if you buy this facial cream or dye your hair this color, you are buying a little of the same magic, and that is where you too can be. Ambition to possess something of that status makes L'Oréal its billions. We easily forget the excellent definition of "ambition" from Ambrose Bierce's *Devil's Dictionary*: "an overmastering desire to be vilified by enemies while living and made ridiculous by friends when dead."

Smith said of our tendency to hero-worship:

> The man of rank and distinction, on the contrary, is observed by all the world. Every body is eager to look at him, and to conceive, at least by sympathy, that joy and exultation with which his circumstances naturally inspire him. His actions are the objects of the public care. Scarce a word, scarce a gesture, can fall from him that is altogether neglected. In a great assembly he is the person upon whom all direct their eyes; it is upon him that their passions seem all to wait with

> expectation, in order to receive that movement and direction which he shall impress upon them; and if his behaviour is not altogether absurd, he has, every moment, an opportunity of interesting mankind, and of rendering himself the object of the observation and fellow-feeling of every body about him. It is this, which, notwithstanding the restraint it imposes, notwithstanding the loss of liberty with which it is attended, renders greatness the object of envy, and compensates, in the opinion of mankind, all that toil, all that anxiety, all those mortifications which must be undergone in the pursuit of it; and what is of yet more consequence, all that leisure, all that ease, all that careless security, which are forfeited for ever by the acquisition.[1]

What Smith calls "a man of rank and distinction" we call a celebrity: the object of all eyes, the people whose words and gestures count. In the eighteenth century, evidently, there was a caveat that to maintain such a position, a person's behavior should be "not altogether absurd." We have lost that, so that the divinity that surrounds our celebrities is scarcely dinted and might even be enhanced by the most absurd behavior: the dimwitted faith in Scientology or the kabbalah, astrology or faith healing, excites the tabloids. Indeed, as I write, celebrity political commentator Bill O'Reilly of Fox News opines that science has no explanation for the movement of the tides, while another celebrity is quoted as saying that she doesn't like the beach, because the salt in the sea is due to its saturation by all that whale sperm. Far from puncturing twenty-first-century celebrity, such idiocy enhances it. But otherwise, Smith is completely right about the effects—envy and forgetfulness—on our off-guard imaginations.

Why forgetfulness? In Smith's view we forget what the "man of distinction" has had to forfeit either to achieve or to maintain his position. We forget the costs and cares to which, like all human beings, he is subject. But I think we also forget that it is not likely that someone should be prone to vanity without also being prone to envy. To understand this, we must first take a detour through the notion of vanity itself. It takes many forms, and it is useful to distinguish two rather different poles around which it can revolve, two different paradigms or models or templates, each of which provide one of its varieties. In one of them it is the kind of disdain that we have been describing: the nose-in-the-air indifference to the sayings, doings, or attitudes of those inferior to oneself. In this form vanity is a sublime conceit, incapable of being dinted or affected by what the world may say. Like Narcissus, its possessor is in effect a psychological solipsist. It is as if the others simply do not exist for them. Their incense is simply her due; it would be their loss, not hers, if they did not supply it.

But the other form is very different. It is an excessive desire for the envy of others. It sucks up praise; it goes out of its way to attract it; it feeds on the superiority to which the first form of vanity is indifferent. It is, in short, a gripping, caustic, obsessive desire—an aching need—for the envy of others. This is what would gratify it, but to be in the grip of this greed requires a lively imagination of that envy, and that in turn could only come from close acquaintance with the vice in oneself. In its first form vanity is cold; in its second form it is hot enough, but extreme and unsatisfiable, and built on this corrosive foundation. Smith thought that this second kind of vanity drove avarice or the greed for money as well:

> From whence, then, arises that emulation which runs through all the different ranks of men, and what are the advantages which we propose by that great purpose of human life which we call bettering our condition? To be observed, to be attended to, to be taken notice of with sympathy, complacency, and approbation, are all the advantages

> which we can propose to derive from it. It is the vanity, not the ease, or the pleasure, which interests us. But vanity is always founded upon the belief of our being the object of attention and approbation. The rich man glories in his riches, because he feels that they naturally draw upon him the attention of the world, and that mankind are disposed to go along with him in all those agreeable emotions with which the advantages of his situation so readily inspire him. At the thought of this, his heart seems to swell and dilate itself within him, and he is fonder of his wealth, upon this account, than for all the other advantages it procures him.[2]

Smith here recognizes what I have called the second variety of vanity, the one that depends on exciting the "attention and approbation" of others. I think the first solipsistic kind exists as well, but undoubtedly the second is much more common than the first; indeed, it is likely that what looks like the first is often just a parade of carelessness undertaken to disguise the hot, inordinate desires that make up the second. We have claimed already that sufficient self-reliance to ignore the herd can be fostered by the right upbringing in the herd, but the process is chancy, and, I suspect, fails more often than it succeeds. The real or imagined voices of others still matter to us. After all, fame lures Dante and Petrarch, and Apollo settles for the laurel wreath in the end. So more often than not the air of indifference is an affectation, disguising a nature riddled with envy for those felt to have more and contempt for those supposed to have less, in whatever scale of values the victim has erected. Often enough then, underneath the pose of indifference, any failure of others to admire us as they should still stings.

The actual model may foolishly attempt to live the life she is paid to project, and risk the fate of Narcissus. But she may equally be a timid, anorexic girl of low self-esteem, pathetically dependent on the envy of others, expressed through the constant flatteries of an army of hairdressers, makeup artists, Photoshoppers, and the rest. The persona in the advertisement is a fiction, a creature of our own imagining, although, of course, our imagination has been very cleverly steered. Like Narcissus, the audience of the advertisement only falls in love with a phantasm, and one that will predictably vanish when they try to possess it. You can only buy the brief illusion that you too deserve to belong with the gods (we see later that Eve herself thought this, briefly but catastrophically). But *that* was not what you thought you were buying when you were told you were worth it, for surely you are worth more than living an illusion, living in a fool's paradise that is soon to turn to ashes? You thought you were pampering yourself, cosseting your own ego, suppressing any fear of inadequacy, by buying a pedestal—but alas, really you were buying Echo's voice, or a few delusive moments by Narcissus's pool.

Apparently the original slogan for L'Oréal had been "Because I'm worth it." I think it was lucky for the company, if not for its customers, that they improved upon this.[3] The fact that the persona in the picture is worth it is a given. It stares us in the face. But that by itself is merely dispiriting. We are already afraid of our inferiority, the way in which our blotches and blemishes mean that we fall short of our ideals. It does not trigger the thought that we too can buy the magic, go to the ball, meet the prince, and live on our pedestal happily ever after. But being told that *we* are worth all that is a different matter. Human beings only have to be told things to half-believe them, and our vanities are evidently always on a hair trigger.

It is no part of this criticism that personal appearance is or should be unimportant. Human beings have always put effort into maintaining it as best they can: mirrors, combs, and adornments have been discovered in burial sites as far back as the Bronze Age. If luck or care deliver a great end result, this is a bonus. Handsome, graceful, glowing, beautiful . . . for those lucky enough to deserve the descriptions, life has a rosy tint. They are, after all, attractive. They find friends more easily, as well as partners. They earn more. Evidence from the United States suggests that handsome men earn, on average, 5 percent more than their less-attractive counterparts, and good-looking women earn 4 percent more. It starts early in life; we smile longer at pretty babies, and pretty students get more attention from teachers:

> Asked to rank employee attributes in order of importance, meanwhile, managers placed looks above education: of nine character traits, it came in third, below experience (No. 1) and confidence (No. 2) but above "where a candidate went to school" (No. 4). Does that mean you should drop out of Harvard and invest in a nose job? Probably not. But a state school might be just as marketable. "This is the new reality of the job market," says one New York recruiter, who asked to have her name withheld because she advises job candidates for a living. "It's better to be average and good-looking than brilliant and unattractive."[4]

No wonder the economy is in a mess. Nor is this bias confined to the somewhat feverish glamour-stricken job market of New York, or even the United States. Physical presence can have the same cachet in many contexts. I once attended a carol service in a great English cathedral, and was much diverted to see that in the stately procession of clerics, the tall, commanding figure of the bishop, magnificent under his towering miter, was followed by a slightly shorter dean, and then in strictly descending order of height came progressively inferior men of God, right down to the assistant curate of some insignificant rural parish, who was practically a midget.

But to return to cosmetics, the unfortunate customer hoping to boost her beauty score does not become the persona in the advertisement. She is no younger, and probably no more attractive—although there may be a small side-effect of increased confidence, which is itself an attractive feature, up to a point. She is certainly no nearer to her dream, so long as she depends on praise and approval and adoration from others when she unveils the cosmetic she has used—and she inevitably will depend on these. In the fantasy, these are in abundant supply, and the mesmerized customer forgets that in the real world, they never are. For other people are their own centers of interest. They do not care very much what the customer looks like; they are far more concerned with how they themselves stand in each other's eyes. Incense remains in short supply. Narcissus is left on his own, and that too was one of the morals of the myth. Why is Narcissus a solitary, if not that his very obsession makes him one, and keeps him being one?

All this may raise the corrosive question whether what we think of as erotic love is always narcissistic, always solitary. In Western art Venus is more often depicted admiring herself than trying to be nice to anybody else. Freud thought that narcissism was the core element in erotic love, and of course the catastrophic wound to the self when such love is betrayed or lost suggests that there is something right about the view. The corrosions of jealousy arise purely from the blow to the self.

The arrogant belief that one is oneself the center of other people's concerns and interest is also the reason why flattery is such a pervasive feature of the social world. One of the earliest of many moralistic laments against the practices of flattery comes in Plato's dialogue *Gorgias*, where Socrates somewhat unconvincingly argues that flattery is to politics what cookery is to medicine or gymnastics. His rather clunky idea seems to have been that we can be deceived by the arts of the cook into thinking we are doing our bodies good by eating things that in fact do us no good; similarly, we can be deceived by the arts of the flatterer into all kinds of false views about our merits.[5] This is obvious enough, although in a democracy I should have thought there are closer links between flattery and politics than that. Without mutual flatteries, neither the candidate nor the electorate are nearly as likely to be deceived as they need to be. In any event, the Renaissance humanist Erasmus nicely voices the other side of the coin:

> True, there is a certain kind of flattery which is altogether destructive, the kind employed by some unprincipled cynics to ruin their wretched victims. But this flattery of mine proceeds from a kind disposition and a certain frankness which is much closer to a virtue than the opposite qualities, "soundness" and "peevishness," "jangling" as Horace says "and dour." This kind of flattery gives a lift to those whose spirits are low, consoles those who mourn, stimulates the apathetic, rouses the dull, cheers the sick, tames the fierce, unites lovers and keeps them united . . . in sum it is the honey and spice of all human intercourse. But to be deceived, they say, is miserable. Quite the contrary not to be deceived is the most miserable of all. For nothing could be further from the truth than the notion that man's happiness resides in things as they actually are. It depends on opinions.[6]

Admittedly, Erasmus is here somewhat heavy-handedly impersonating Folly, or the spirit of foolishness, but there is a lot that is recognizable, and something that is right in what he imagines Folly saying. Folly and we are well acquainted, after all.

It can be amazingly difficult to remember that other people are not primarily bothered about *me* but about themselves. Seeing me on a pedestal does not provoke, as I might incautiously suppose, Smith's "admiration and applause." It is far more likely to provoke indifference at best; envy, malice, and ridicule at worst. But self-conceit forbids us from recognizing this. Traits other than arrogance can prompt the same preoccupation. Adolescents especially, preoccupied with their own lives not through arrogance but through insecurity, are often incapable of realizing that they are not the primary object of the concerns, opinions, and criticisms of everybody, and it is their resistance to this understanding that makes their self-consciousness so painful and paralyzing. The fearful and fragile situation of a lover turns grown adults into adolescents in just this respect. Jean-Jacques Rousseau gives a charming example of this in the course of distinguishing between courtesy, which can and should be shown to everybody, and coquetry, which requires dividing and conquering. So a clever woman with two suitors will not treat them alike:

> Oh, she is far too clever for that; so far from treating them just alike she makes a marked difference between them, and she does it so skillfully that the man she flatters thinks it is affection, and the man she ill uses thinks it is spite. So that each of them believes she is thinking of him, when she is thinking of no one but herself.[7]

So, alas, people do not fall over in love and admiration when you buy the new lipstick. They have their own lives to live. The magic doesn't work, and the consumer inevitably fails. But in her imagination, the solution may be—to try again! Harder! Perhaps the next facial cream or lipstick, hair color or self-tanning gel, will do the trick. If pampering the self does not work at first, try it again. Do it more thoroughly, whatever it costs. And so a dismal, infinite regress of unfulfilled hopes, discontent, and disappointment opens in front of the poor supplicant, but a nice infinite regress of profit for the supplier. One wants to shout that the deluded customer can and should think of herself as worth more than the haggard chaser of illusions that she risks becoming, but one's voice is unlikely to compete with the illusions.

As already hinted, it is wrong to jump to the conclusion that it is always vanity that is at work here. It may be fear, and is often a simple need for self-respect. We all like to keep up appearances. As Cicero insisted, dignity and decorum are part of the social world; we naturally wash and put on our clothes and our manners to deal with one another. Hence, a serious deformity or blemish that ruins our appearance may well assault our sense of self, our ability to bear our own survey of our own lives. Disfigurements are terrible, and wanting reconstruction to rectify such things would be open signals of sociability or a desire to return properly into human society. They are an attempt to open the door into the social world, when the door has been shut by accident or misfortune, and hence, a kind of overture that invites a reciprocal return from others. It is like employing a mouthwash if you fear that you suffer from Hume's "stinking breath." It can be an instance of pride rather than vanity, and pride as well in its most admirable form, of giving us the courage to deal with adversity.

So I doubt if cosmetic surgical enhancements (as opposed to reconstructions) rely on exactly the same advertising dynamic as more mundane cosmetic applications. On the face of it one might have expected the advertisements for these gross procedures to stress the inadequacies of the patient more than the divinity of the end product. It seems, to me at least, surprising that pursuit of a phantom ideal could be strong enough to lure people into operating rooms, whereas I can well imagine that obsession with their own inadequacies, shame, or low self-esteem might push them there. Perhaps it is not so much the glamour of "because I'm worth it" as the abasement of "because I am worth nothing" that propels people to the surgeons.

And this unlocked the key, to me, of the problem I mentioned in the preface: my inchoate despair at L'Oréal. I came to understand that the underlying message was not "because you're worth it" but "because you aren't worth it. But you could be if you buy the stuff." The whole allure, the glamour, the dazzle rested on a dissonance between what the customer is being told and what she will feel like on being told it, which is the exact opposite. "I myself am but a poor worm," thinks the victim, "with warts and fat and farts and fears. But L'Oréal will waft me away, take me up to the empyrean, the other world where the royalty—no, the gods—live free from mortal woes and flaws and worries and . . ." It is subliminally putting the bulk of humanity into the same pit of fear and despair that, more understandably, threatens to afflict those who do find themselves shameful, or inadequate, or unable to face the gaze of their fellows.

It is no credit to our phase of civilization if it is fear rather than ambition that drives most of those who bankrupt themselves on the vanities, or who end up under the surgeon's knife. It is the fear of falling short, of being inadequate in the eyes of others, including loved ones. It is the sense that without the right shape of this bit, or less or more of that other bit, one is going to be inadequate in other people's eyes. It is desperately sad that quite normal people suffer these fears, and one can certainly moralize about the ways in which the demand for the perfect body has been implanted and inflated by the cosmetic surgery industry, in an unholy alliance with the world of fashion and the magic of Photoshop. This is not to blame the victims, for their anxieties are real enough, even if they are the result of wholly discreditable pressures.

Objectified and valued only for appearance, women especially (but men as well) become afraid and desperate when their sense of their own appearance is poor and, with age perhaps, getting poorer. Once people are commodified, valuable in their own eyes only to the extent to which their appearance is imagined to be valued by others, they become enslaved by this fear, and a whole world of pain, desperation, and misery opens up. For confirmation of this dynamic, consider that more than 3,200,000 hopefuls in the United States alone went voluntarily under the plastic surgeon's knife in 2010, while between 400,000 and 500,000 women in France have had breast implants (yet one always thought Frenchwomen were so chic, so confident). A recent scandal in which faulty silicone turned out to have been provided to 30,000 of them brought out the grim stories:

> "I've always suffered from depression and mental-health problems linked to body image," said the 48-year-old from Normandy. "I earn €1,000 [£840 or $1,300] a month in a factory. I couldn't afford breast surgery until my late 40s. But after the implants I felt better, I came off the antidepressants, I was able to face work. Then I find out the implants are poison. The tests say they're still in place but I'm having

> them removed anyway. I'm terrified they'll rupture or explode at any moment.
>
> "I try to sleep on my back, if I sleep at all. Some people try to avoid extreme physical exercise for fear of damaging the implants, but I do hard labour on a factory line.
>
> "I go to bed feeling bad, I wake up feeling bad. It's like living with a ticking bomb inside you."

If this is simply sad, one might feel less charitable to anyone who knows that they are normal, or even better than normal, but wants the surgeons to make them better still. Nobody should want that delusive pedestal, nor want to listen obsessively to their own voice telling them either flattering or less than flattering stories about their superiorities to others. Nobody should want a free ticket to these exercises of vanity and arrogance. In these less forgivable cases, it is surely a lapse from restraint, or dignity and decorum, to go to a surgeon for trivial cosmetic reasons. It is unfitting, one might say, improper, treating one's own body as a tool rather than a part of oneself. It is a horrific example of greed for the envy of others.

The bottom line is that it dishonors ourselves, for we ought to think better of ourselves than that. And once we are caught in the coils of the serpent, it may be almost impossible to get out of them. For, as a species of greed, it shares with monetary greed the problem that we soon explore, that its ambitions are never satisfied.

But isn't there a villainous Edward Hyde inside the most respectable and benevolent Henry Jekyll? Is there a tiny yet insistent voice asking whether it wouldn't be nice to have all the enviable attributes of a trophy wife or husband or partner, and on top of it not to care what anybody else thought? Wouldn't it be nice to be obeyed when we demand that others think little of themselves in comparison with us—forgetting Kant's warning that the demand is always unsatisfied? How heavenly to be Narcissus freed from his solitary state but the object of envy and desire to an adoring public. L'Oréal probably had no intention of confirming the deep truth of the Greek myth, but the company could scarcely have done so more effectively.

4

Hubris and the Fragile Self

A sense of our own standing or self-worth is a moral stance or disposition. It refers, at least in part, to what we feel we deserve from other people, by way of deference, esteem, or admiration. Yet psychologists who study what are known as narcissistic personality disorders sharply distinguish between those and real self-esteem. Indeed, paradoxically, this kind of narcissism is well seen as the result of especially *low* self-esteem. It is because this kind of narcissist's self-esteem is so low that their personality becomes fragile, overdependent on the opinion of others, and that they are quick to resort to anger, aggression, despair, or paranoia when that praise falls into short supply.

Hence, the narcissist in the psychological literature is not particularly close to the boy in the Greek myth, nor to the poor customer seduced by the cosmetics industry into paying some absurd sum for little or no benefit. In one description he suffers from "grandiose feelings possibly arising from fragile self-esteem, impairment in interpersonal relations, a sense of entitlement, the belief that one's problems or one's successes are unique, constant need for attention and admiration and an exaggerated sense of failure when something goes wrong." Narcissus suffered from some of these. His personal relations were nonexistent, and he constantly needed his own admiration. But he is not credited with a sense of entitlement. Precisely because he is so solitary, locked into his own mental world, he makes no demands on others, and has no sense of grievance when others fail to play their part. He felt grief at the inaccessible nature of the object of his love, but we are not told that he translated that into an exaggerated sense of his own failure. So the modern narcissist has quite a lot of extra baggage on board.

Psychologists have similarly distinguished four different dimensions of narcissism:

Leadership/Authority (enjoying being a leader and being seen as an authority)
Self-Absorption/Self-Admiration (admiring one's own physical appearance and personality)
Superiority/Arrogance (overestimation of one's own abilities, underlying themes of superiority and grandiosity), and finally
Exploitativeness/Entitlement (interpersonal manipulation, expectations of favors, exploitation of others).

Again, the boy in the myth scored highly only on the second of these, although in his indifference to other people there are hints of the third. But there is no suggestion that he enjoyed being a leader, was exploitative in his dealings with others, or expected much of them. Furthermore, there are surely people naturally described as narcissists who suffer from the first kind of vanity—disdain and indifference to others, cocooned in their own bloated self-conceit—rather than the second, in which they are pathetically dependent on constant reaffirmation from others.

Nevertheless, it is easy to believe that these traits often go together, reinforcing each other and thereby forming a natural cluster. It is also easy to believe that they usually betoken an underlying failure of self-esteem. Someone only needs constant reaffirmation from others if they have insufficient self-confidence or self-esteem to "go it alone" or show a genuine self-reliance.

> A grandiose yet vulnerable self-concept . . . underlies the chronic goal of obtaining continuous external self-affirmation. Because narcissists are insensitive to others' concerns and social constraints and view others as inferior, their self-regulatory efforts often are counterproductive and ultimately prevent the positive feedback that they seek—thus undermining the self that they are trying to create and maintain.[1]

This is what Kant described slightly more elegantly as "a foolishness that acts contrary to its own end," or the hellish structure of "odi et amo"—I hate and I love. The narcissist is here pictured as chronically dependent on the praise of the very people whom he wants to consider inferior and worthless, just as the doomed lover may need the constant flattery of a partner that he or she also considers inferior, or even despicable. He or she cannot do without the flattery, but because despising those who offer it, finds that the offering turns to ashes. The cosmetics consumer is in the same cleft stick: odi et amo. Her sense of independence is itself utterly dependent on the admiration of precisely those others whom she wished to surpass, and in a sense annihilate.

Why do people become like that? Here are the outlines of a popular story. The newborn infant has no sense of the distinction between itself and other things. It has no self-consciousness, no awareness of the difference between the world as it is and the experiences that it has. The gradual dawning of the distinction between itself and its world comes only after it has organized its perceptual experience and begun to adapt itself to the fact that it is situated in an environment that it can change in some ways but not in others. At this stage, it is often supposed, any resistance to its own wishes and its own will is construed as enemy action, as a cause of distress and rage. It is as if it personifies the physical forces that constrain it or that frustrate or deny its needs and desires as direct personal challenges to its will: resistance is an injustice, a malign object of resentment and grievance. This is why babies are so often angry.

But as it matures, it begins to separate the world within which it has to move from the things it can alter. Some resistances become just the way things are rather than anything about which to get worked up. It also learns of the existence of others: the mother or carer who is a welcome bearer of love and support but who, inexplicably, can also resist even the most imperious demands of the will. If things go well, all this comes into a kind of adjustment, but it is not difficult to see that the process leaves legacies, and can go wrong.

Suppose, for example, the baby has a mother too absorbed in her own life to give it due care and attention, love and security. It learns that it must cope with a loveless world, and it is not difficult to see how this would affect its sense of self for the worse. Insecure, it finds it easy to hate rivals for the affection of which it is being starved. Angry, aggrieved, wary, it might remain quick to interpret resistance as injustice. Or it may be drawn to the arts of manipulation, of wheedling and fawning and appearing other than it is. An exaggerated sense of what is owing to it might be perceived, unconsciously, as the only way of getting what is in fact owing to it. And so the tyrannical or narcissistic or manipulative self that the psychologists describe is built on the foundation of insecurity and need.

I like this story, but I am not particularly wedded to it. Such constructions are almost inevitably speculative, although some may strike us as more plausible and convincing than others. But they are bound to be interpretations of a poor data set, for the ways people grow up are very different, and there is a large distance between the infant's observed states and any theory of its thinking about the world and its place in it. Shakespeare's Julius Caesar said that there is no art to tell the mind's construction from the face. He was exaggerating: in the case of those we know well and whom we trust, we can do this with ease and certainty. You can see just by looking that your partner is finding something distasteful or amusing, interesting or boring. And even in less secure cases, we are skilled at detecting the fake rictus that is not a genuine smile, or the insincerity in a voice. But he was nearer to being right when it comes to telling the mind of the baby from its face. And when the baby's mind is being invested with moral notions (such as grievance, injustice, resentment, desert, insult) that imply a distinct sense of the self and what is owed to it, we have to worry whether we are simply projecting adult feelings onto a creature that is as yet incapable of sharing them. The baby mind is not too subtle, but too simple for us to enter into it.

Remembering Collingwood's insight, we may want to say that at this stage the infant has not discovered itself at all, rather than that it has done so and believes itself to be a monarch or dictator.

So there is something unhappy about reinterpreting the infant's lack of a distinction between itself and the world into a sense that it is itself the whole world, that it itself rules omnipotent. For that must seem to imply an exaggerated conception of itself, whereas it is more natural to deny it any consciousness of self at all (it is more like the aged victim of dementia than a genuinely self-conscious adolescent). It is also odd to invest it with moral notions, yet construing the resistances the world offers as occasions for indignation and resentment seems to suggest just that. As we shall see later, these are complex mental states, implying a sense of having been belittled, or treated unjustly, or denied a proper dignity. Yet there is no independent evidence that at the earliest stages of life the infant has the ability to deploy these concepts. It is too much a creature of sensation, and too little a creature of thought. It is too early for its own status to preoccupy it, and for slights to that status to shock it.

Infants are certainly angry often enough. But their anger is better seen not as an expression of resentment or moral outrage, but rather as one of distress, of finding a discomfort and being unable to do anything except to signal it, rather as a lonely dog similarly howls in distress. Admittedly, to an adult, an expression of distress and one of anger are not the same thing. But the current of life runs more lustily in the infant. It is not possible for an infant to express distress by sullen silence, or despair, at least until things are truly terrible and the current of life is beginning to fade.

A story about the etiology of narcissism probably gets onto firmer ground when we contemplate the many wrong kinds of ways in which children may be brought up, and the fragile self that is likely to emerge from some of them. The origins of narcissism sit more comfortably in this longer time frame. When we expand our gaze to include the whole process of growing through childhood, we should also expand it beyond the microenvironment of family and siblings. The pervasive powers of culture, in the shape of scripts and templates telling the child how to behave, what is expected, what little boys do and don't do, and little girls likewise, crowd in to mold, and often enough warp, the emerging personality. We may not be wedded to Wordsworth's Romantic belief that heaven lies about us in our infancy. But we can be certain that shades of the prison house begin to close soon enough. And there are enough pitfalls on their journey to the prison house of character or personality to make many an adult fragile, insecure, envious, or vain. The child's journey is upon a tightrope, and many things—too much praise, too little praise; too much success, too little success; too much competition, too little competition—may be enough to push him or her into the abyss.

It is time to confess that the narcissist is frequently charming. He sets out to be, since he has learned that this is the surest way to harvest good opinion, or at least the appearance of it. And his apparent self-confidence may be infectious. It is only when we penetrate the mask and find that he does not care a fig about us, but only about himself, that disillusion sets in. The author Alan Bennett puts it especially nicely, describing one of his characters:

> One does not have to be in the forefront of the struggle for women's rights to find Betty's decision to marry Graham deplorable. She wasn't wholly infatuated, although she liked the way he looked; but so too did he, and that unfatuated her a bit.[2]

Narcissism is closely allied with demented self-confidence: hubris. In his book *The Hubris Syndrome: Bush, Blair and the Intoxication of*

Power, the politician and medical doctor David Owen suggests that "there is a pattern of hubristic behavior manifest in some leaders, particularly political leaders, which could legitimately be deemed to constitute a medically recognized syndrome," which he calls the hubristic syndrome. It afflicts some political leaders, but not all. Owen believes that it derives from some kind of narcissistic personality disorder, but goes beyond that. Its consequences throughout human history have been disastrous. Owen suggests that a sprinkling of behavioral symptoms from the following list characterizes the disorder:

—A narcissistic propensity to see the world primarily as an arena in which they can exercise power and seek glory rather than as a place with problems that need approaching in a pragmatic and non-self-referential manner;
—a predisposition to take actions which seem likely to cast them in a good light—i.e., in order to enhance their image;
—a disproportionate concern with image and presentation;
—a messianic manner of talking about what they are doing and a tendency to exaltation;
—an identification of themselves with the state to the extent that they regard the outlook and interests of the two as identical;
—a tendency to talk of themselves in the third person or using the royal "we";
—excessive confidence in their own judgment and contempt for the advice or criticism of others;
—exaggerated self-belief, bordering on a sense of omnipotence, in what they personally can achieve;
—a belief that rather than being accountable to the mundane court

of colleagues or public opinion, the real court to which they answer is much greater: History or God;

—an unshakeable belief that in that court they will be vindicated;

—restlessness, recklessness, and impulsiveness;

—a tendency to allow their "broad vision," especially their conviction about the moral rectitude of a proposed course of action, to obviate the need to consider other aspects of it, such as its practicality, cost, and the possibility of unwanted outcomes;

—a consequent type of incompetence in carrying out a policy, which could be called hubristic incompetence. This is where things go wrong precisely because too much self-confidence has led the leader not to bother worrying about the nuts and bolts of a policy. It can be allied to an incurious nature.[3]

Owen details the way in which George Bush Jr., and more especially Tony Blair, eventually checked all these sinister boxes as their period in power unfolded. Margaret Thatcher had previously become another victim, and history shows many precursors.

Excessive self-confidence is easily engendered by early success, particularly if that success was achieved while acting against the advice of others. All our personalities are refined by practice, and if nature unkindly gives us practice at trusting our own judgment above that of others, and at reaping success and applause because of it, she is sowing the seeds of eventual hubris. But nature can sow the seeds another way as well. We are good at deceiving ourselves about our own merits, and only need to *believe* that we have done better than others to become satisfied that this is what we are like. It is as if when it comes to failures, we coat ourselves in Teflon and they do not stick, whereas our supposed successes sit firmly in our memory bank. We also give different kind of attention to successes and to failures. The former are due to ourselves; the latter due to bad luck. Psychologists speak here of self-serving biases, or the self-attribution fallacy: the tendency to take personal credit for perceived successes while at the same time shunting off responsibility for apparent failures elsewhere. It was the situation, the bad advice of others, the inadequate instruments, the sheer bad luck.

Christian moralists were here before modern psychologists. Pride, in Christian thought, is frequently associated with a delusive belief in *self-sufficiency*, an attempt to see oneself as having the same kind of independence of the world and other people that is only properly ascribed to God. God is unique in being *causa sui*, his own cause, but we are dependent on chance, gifts of fortune, other people, the contingencies of the world, and, of course, eventually on God himself. Forgetting this is the root of all evil.

> For thou hast said in thine heart, I will ascend into heaven, I will exalt my throne above the stars of God: I will sit also upon the mount of the congregation . . . .[4]

As we see later, one of the potent temptations that Satan offers Eve is to get out from under obedience to arbitrary contingency, and to ascend to a more godlike independence. In some Christian moralists, such as Saint Augustine, even ascribing some good to our own "unaided" efforts is a temptation of pride. We must remember instead that what we ascribe to our own will or our own virtue, if it is at all good, is nothing but the working of grace inside us, and is therefore entirely due to God. Or, as we might put it in a secular age, everything about ourselves (including, for instance, our ability to withstand temptation or to exercise resolution or perseverance in any task) is due to natural forces that have worked on us and shaped us from outside. We should no more take credit for them, and become bigheaded because of them, than we should take credit for the color of our eyes or the shape of our bones.[5] It is luck, good or bad, all the way down. But just try getting the hubristic leader, or the successful businessman, or this season's new film star, puffed out with his or her own self-belief, to accept that.

It may seem strange that anyone with even incipient tendencies toward the hubristic syndrome should ever manage to impose upon others and gain business success or electoral success. But, of course, as with the narcissistic personality, self-confidence is in itself an attractive trait, at least at first. In a remarkable study, psychologists Belinda Board and Katarina Fritzon compared a group of senior business managers to three groups of patients, including groups incarcerated in Broadmoor, the most serious psychiatric detention center in the UK:

> The results here confirm the presence of elements of PD (personality disorder) in the senior business manager sample, and those most prominent are among those most associated with psychopathic PD. Relative to the three patient samples, particularly the PPD (psychiatric personality disorder) and MI (mental illness) patient samples, the senior business manager group is more likely to demonstrate the traits associated with histrionic PD, and equally likely to demonstrate the traits associated with narcissistic and compulsive PDs. At a descriptive level this translates to: superficial charm, insincerity, egocentricity, manipulativeness (histrionic), grandiosity, lack of empathy, exploitativeness, independence (narcissistic), perfectionism, excessive

> devotion to work, rigidity, stubbornness, and dictatorial tendencies (compulsive). Conversely, the senior business manager group is less likely to demonstrate physical aggression, consistent irresponsibility with work and finances, lack of remorse (antisocial), impulsivity, suicidal gestures, affective instability (borderline), mistrust (paranoid), and hostile defiance alternated with contrition (passive/aggressive).[6]

Perhaps the biggest surprise here is that aggression, lack of remorse, and financial irresponsibility have their volume turned *down* in senior business managers. We might have predicted the reverse. But we must remember that this is only by comparison with people who have actually been locked up for antisocial and dangerous behavior. Compared to normal members of the population, they may be well up the scale here as well.

There is also considerable overlap between the hubristic person and the charismatic. The same messianic self-belief, the promise of carrying his supporters ever forward to the brightest future, the demonization of critics, and the unshakeable self-righteousness can intoxicate the audience just as much as the victim himself. In time, inevitably, disillusion sets in and the audience applause is replaced with not only disappointment but a sense of betrayal, a bitter and often angry consciousness of having been duped.

Hubris is, or should be, followed by nemesis, the just retribution that reality inflicts on those who care less about it than they do about themselves. Unfortunately, nemesis often appears to have a very poor aim, and the catastrophes that hubris brings about fall on other people, while the hubristic leader bows himself off the stage with his vast pension pot or his immortal memory embodied in a statue erected by a grateful nation. Meanwhile, his colossal self-belief, sense of righteousness, sense of omnipotence, and often sense of grievance at having been replaced or undervalued remain utterly unscathed. It is an unjust world, and this is one very galling example of it.

Or is it? The hubristic man puts on a show, but can he really bear his own company? In the dark hours, when self-knowledge tussles with self-deception, does the worm of doubt devour him? We might like to think so. After all, if the root was narcissism, then just as the narcissistic person needs to think that he has the constant attention and apparent affection of others, so does the charismatic. When the electorate feels betrayed, it is not going to give that. It wants something entirely different from the onetime idol, namely, contrition and apology. The man of hubris, who answers only to History or to God, is not going to give that: "Hey, let's just move on, all right?" The evils he does must be brushed aside, or, what is worse, reinterpreted in terms of justified resentment against the very people whom he has done down. Such evils are always the fault of those on whom the hubristic leader inflicts them. If people had just been more resolute in following him (or her), none of this would have happened.

But by his immunity to contrition, the narcissistic or hubristic agent meets our resentment. For as Smith admirably put it:

> The object . . . which resentment is chiefly intent upon, is not so much to make our enemy feel pain in his turn, as to make him conscious that he feels it upon account of his past conduct, to make him repent of that conduct, and to make him sensible, that the person whom he injured did not deserve to be treated in that manner. What chiefly enrages us against the man who injures or insults us, is the little account which he seems to make of us, the unreasonable preference which he gives to himself above us, and that absurd self-love, by which

> he seems to imagine, that other people may be sacrificed at any time, to his conveniency or his humour. The glaring impropriety of this conduct, the gross insolence and injustice which it seems to involve in it, often shock and exasperate us more than all the mischief which we have suffered. To bring him back to a more just sense of what is due to other people, to make him sensible of what he owes us, and of the wrong that he has done to us, is frequently the principal end proposed in our revenge, which is always imperfect when it cannot accomplish this. When our enemy appears to have done us no injury, when we are sensible that he acted quite properly, that, in his situation, we should have done the same thing, and that we deserved from him all the mischief we met with; in that case, if we have the least spark either of candour or justice, we can entertain no sort of resentment.[7]

We return later to the way in which resentment seeks to balance things out, redress something that has gone out of kilter, in connection with Kant. Here the point is that it is doubly galling when the hubristic agent refuses the recognition and reparation that we believe we deserve. First he duped us, and now he insults us. We hope that in his innermost being his misdeeds weigh more heavily upon him than he allows us to see. And perhaps they do. There are often those telltale signs of stress: the twitch in the eye, the impatience, the trembling hand. Jean-Jacques Rousseau, a skilled dissector of the human soul, thought this would always be so, so that the villain is more properly an object of pity than hatred, although when our own self-interest is involved, we are unlikely to see that it is so:

> We are aware of the offence, but we do not see the punishment; the advantages are plain, the penalty is hidden. The man who thinks he is

> enjoying the fruits of his vices is no less tormented by them than if they had not been successful; the object is different, the anxiety is the same; in vain he displays his good fortune and hides his heart; in spite of himself his conduct betrays him; but to discern this, our own heart must be utterly unlike his.[8]

Smith took the same line:

> Amidst all the gaudy pomp of the most ostentatious greatness; amidst the venal and vile adulation of the great and of the learned; amidst the more innocent, though more foolish, acclamations of the common people; amidst all the pride of conquest and the triumph of successful war, he is still secretly pursued by the avenging furies of shame and remorse; and, while glory seems to surround him on all sides, he himself, in his own imagination, sees black and foul infamy fast pursuing him, and every moment ready to overtake him from behind.[9]

Yet I fear that both philosophers exaggerate, for I do not believe we can rule out villains who are annoyingly unconscious of their villainy or even, heaven help us, annoyingly cheerful about it. A continuing hubristic personality may inhabit a self-protective cocoon of his own fantasy, but worse even than this are people who positively take pride in doing others down, in having got away with it, perhaps in the conviction that everyone would be like them if they were as clever and courageous as they are. As David Hume, judicious as ever, pointed out, "a sense of shame, in an imperfect character, is certainly a virtue; but produces great uneasiness and remorse, from which the abandoned villain is entirely free."

Nevertheless, there certainly may be symptoms of the stress of "being in denial." One is the emphasis on subjective certainty, the self-righteous or self-pitying insistence that "I did what I thought was right," when the finger of the world is pointed not at whether that is true—it well might be, as it was doubtless true of many of history's greatest criminals—but at whether hubris had led the leader to believe he was right when better judgment should have prevailed. Failing to look harder, failing to weigh evidence carefully, failing to think about the long-term and to consider the alternatives, failing to invite skeptics to the table or critics to the conference are moral faults deriving from the need to preserve a fragile sense of security and a self-induced sense of omnipotence. The narcissistic personality sees ordinary life as full of threats and slights, and in the hubristic leader, this means seeing evidence and qualifications and reflection as threatening and dangerous: he wants to "trust his gut" or just "go for it," convinced that his powers will open the way to success. His self-esteem requires decisiveness, or, if we prefer it, thoughtlessness, and in retrospect it requires denial of the moral fault that led to the necessary thought not taking place.

This introduces an explanation of why in George Bush's White House it was a sign of weakness to belong to the "reality-based community," such as, for instance, the community of people who might have doubts about whether Iraq would become a paradise after the US invasion in 2003. But many people can only preserve their balance in a simple world, amenable to simple moral recipes, so that their outrage and incomprehension find suitable targets. As I write, it is still fashionable for successful Republican politicians to sneer at "facts" and "data." Surprisingly, like some of their most hated opponents—left-wing liberal, academic, wishy-washy, hairy, besandaled vegetarians and their ilk—they can only use these words "sous rature," as French philosophers have christened it (roughly, at the same time crossing it out or, as we might say, in inverted commas). But as both camps would be pleased to hear, there is a difference. The philosophes, postmodernists, and in general those on the left use the inverted commas because they revel in the multiple interpretations of things and events that reflection inevitably throws up, and dislike the idea that there is just one true way of looking at things. But for the Republican mind-set, it is just the opposite. Words like "fact" imply a nasty recalcitrance, bringing with them a risk that the world is not the simple cut-and-dried, black-and-white world about which they can lay down the law. Facts turn into inadmissible specters of fallibility, or vulnerability to a world that may not respond properly to whichever simplistic and self-serving dogma has taken hold, be it on poverty, war, immigration, penal policy, energy, abortion, taxes, or the definition of pizza as a vegetable in school meals. Again, there is a denial of contingency, happenstance, or vulnerability: godlike self-sufficiency is here translated into impregnable certainties and dogmas. The workings of pride are many-faceted.

So we might begin to sympathize with Christian moralists who very early cemented into place the idea of pride as the root and foundation of all sins (although this primacy is much less clear in the Hebrew Bible). Here is Gregory the Great, following a line stretching from Origen through Cassian, Ambrose, and Augustine:

> For to all who swell with proud thoughts there is a noisiness in their speech, bitterness in their silence, dissoluteness in their mirth; wrath in their sorrow, unsteadiness in their conduct, comeliness in their appearance, erectness in their gait, rancor in their reply. Their mind is ever strong in inflicting, weak in enduring, contumely; sluggish in

> obeying; importunate in provoking, others; slothful in those things which it ought and has the power, to do, but ready for those which it neither ought, nor is able to do.[10]

Although we have to qualify our acceptance of this. A comely appearance and erect gait don't strike us as vices today, although they can certainly disguise others.

How are we to protect ourselves against the hubris syndrome in politicians? We can certainly be on the lookout for it (the satirical magazine *Private Eye* spotted Tony Blair's messianic tendencies as soon as he became prime minister, christening him "the Vicar of Albion" when most of the British public were still infatuated with him). We can hope that the messianic figure is surrounded not by sycophants and courtiers, but by people strong enough to stand up to him, or her. But the most important thing is a constitutional design ensuring that even those at the top cannot run away from scrutiny and the judgment of others. Narcissus could not stop looking at himself, but the hubristic leader needs to be forced to look at himself more, provided that he or she can do so without falling in love all over again.

5

Self-Esteem, Amour Propre, Pride

If hubris is so dangerous, it would also seem dangerous to encourage it by protecting and boosting self-esteem. Yet high self-esteem is often presented as desirable, and its opposite, low self-esteem, is widely regarded as a cause for pity and concern. High self-esteem is often vaguely thought of as a psychological warm bath in which some people pleasantly luxuriate all the time. Furthermore, the "self-esteem movement" of the late twentieth century promised unlimited benefits from the provision of this warm bath: almost all human flaws, including educational failure, violence, crime, delinquency, failed relationships, depression, drug dependencies, and eating disorders, were the result of low self-esteem and therefore could be alleviated or cured entirely by sufficient injections of the real thing. The State of California even initiated the Task Force on Self-Esteem and Personal and Social Responsibility, hoping both to diminish expensive social problems and to increase its tax take, on the grounds that people with high self-esteem earn more, and therefore pay more tax. One can see why the double benefit of fewer social problems and a higher tax income proved irresistible to so many politicians.

Yet the self-esteem movement has never had a solid empirical basis, and research in the area is bedeviled by many factors. For instance, insofar as measures of self-esteem rely on self-report, they are muddied by the propensity of persons of low self-esteem to report the opposite, and vice versa. And then self-esteem is and presumably ought to be domain specific, so there is no single quality being measured. I might have a relatively high opinion of myself as a professor, but it would be madness for me to have a high opinion of myself as a violinist or golfer.

This introduces an important point about the notion of esteem. The root idea is that of an estimate or valuation, and that reminds us that there are two ways of going wrong: one can value something more than it deserves, or less than it deserves, and in most contexts each kind of mistake can bring its penalties. If I suppose that something is more valuable than it is, I incur various costs, and equally if I undervalue it. The art, then, is normally to value things according to their merits. Why should it be any different when it comes to oneself? If I value myself too highly in some respect, I risk being rebuffed more often than I expected; if I value myself too lowly, I risk passing over as beyond me opportunities from which I could have benefited. Getting it right would seem to be as important here as anywhere else.

So perhaps we should not be surprised that overall increases in self-esteem are of little or no benefit, although it took academic psychology a while to come to terms with this. It took a trawl through an initial haul of around 15,000 academic papers on the subject for psychologists to determine that the only reliable effect that it has is on a subject's reported happiness. But that is itself hardly surprising, for how well we feel about ourselves is certainly a large component in how well we feel about the way things are going for us, which is pretty nearly synonymous with our state of happiness. We quoted Erasmus saying as much in chapter 3: self-esteem "makes everyone more agreeable and likeable to himself, and this is the main ingredient in happiness." It is slightly alarming that a mountain of academic effort succeeded only in bringing forth this mouse of a result. Finding that self-esteem is a component of happiness is no more surprising than finding that self-confidence is a component of audacity. Other correlations either work the other way around (for instance, the high self-esteem is a consequence of the high earnings) or may be the joint result of an antecedent cause (a good education may lead both to reasonable self-satisfaction and high earnings).[1] And sometimes high self-esteem increases bad behavior, such as aggression toward out-groups or a propensity to see oneself as having been slighted, with consequent aggression toward the supposed cause. So California's initiative faltered and died, although its specter haunts innumerable self-help books and educational tracts. Reminding oneself constantly that on every day in every way I am getting better and better is still prescribed as the royal road to worldly success and happiness. Injuring a child's self-esteem is widely regarded as appallingly cruel, while preserving it in happy consciousness of its own perfection is the duty of every parent and every teacher. It is, perhaps, a rare sign of justice in this world that the parents and teachers have to live with the results.

It is tempting to suppose that psychology's failed efforts largely derived from a failure to recognize the contextual and evaluative nature of the notion of esteem. Self-esteem is not a single warm bath with a single temperature measure. It is at best an aggregate of a whole different raft of specific valuations of one's own abilities, achievements, talents, or capacities. This aggregate may be closely related to a general tendency to overconfidence, and we have already met the hubristic leader and his blithe self-certainty. But it is a mistake to see overconfidence always as a vice wholly engendered either by pride or by the fragile or narcissistic self. It can go on without any overt or conscious reference to the self at all. Even Iris Murdoch's humble saint must have confidence that she can do some things and not do others, and her lack of self-consciousness could perfectly well go along with an overconfidence in her various abilities, or high self-esteem. But overconfidence also belongs to almost all of us, or at least far more of us than ever become victims of hubris or narcissistic personality disorders. Surveys constantly show our disproportionate confidence: in one, 95 percent of British drivers rated themselves above average drivers; in another, 94 percent of college professors rated themselves as better than average college professors. People say they are 100 percent confident of being right on tests on which they are in fact right only 78 percent of the time.[2]

And this plays havoc in many contexts. Take this last figure, and consider a building contract with penalty clauses for overrunning the time of a job. Any number of things might delay work and trigger the penalties, so let us imagine four of them: bad enough weather, failed deliveries, a workers' strike, or unforeseen hazards on the site. Suppose that each of these is quite improbable. Sticking with the figure given above, suppose each has a chance of only 22 percent, and that they are independent of one another, meaning that none of them makes any of the others more or less likely. And suppose the contractor, looking at each of them, is not 78 percent certain, but 100 percent certain that it will not happen. With this confidence, he can gaily sign up to quite draconian penalties if the work runs over, since he is sure that it will not. Yet on these figures it is a good deal more probable than not that this will happen—63 percent probable in fact. In other words, the work will be delayed and the penalty will need to be paid in more than three cases out of five. People in all walks of life—not only financial advisers and bankers, but doctors and engineers—have been shown to display frightening inabilities to understand this, and hence frightening degrees of overconfidence. It is as if uncertainty is painful, and we do what we can to suppress it.

The well-known "base rate fallacy" may itself be a creature of overconfidence. A standard illustration comes from medicine. We imagine a relatively rare disease or condition: say, one in a thousand of a population may suffer from it. We then have a test that is billed as highly reliable. If you have the disease, it says that you have it; if you don't, it very seldom—in around 1 percent of cases—gives a false positive and says that you do have it. You test, and alas, it shows that you have it. This is bad news, but how bad? Experienced doctors, just as much as laypeople, judge it is very bad, even that you are pretty certain to have the disease. But that is quite wrong: on these figures, your chance of having the problem is approximately one in eleven. You are still way more likely to be free of it (work it out: for a thousand people tested, one will have the disease, and he will test positive. So will around ten others, since we know that there are about 1 percent of false positives. So out of eleven positives, only one is correctly diagnosed). One way of explaining why people are prone to this fallacy is because of overconfidence: doctors inhabit a world of tests, and reliable tests are a good thing; pride in the white-coated, clinical world of evidence-based medicine requires that you recognize that they are good (and it is true—but not that good). But it is plausible to suggest that this confidence or pride deflects attention from the other elephant in the room: the low base rate and corresponding improbability of the diagnosis. People similarly overestimate the efficacy of both orthodox medicines and quack cures, because they forget the other elephant in the room, which is that most illnesses get better of their own accord. It wasn't the pharmacist's elixir or an overdose of vitamin C that effected the cure but time.

Overconfidence shows itself as well in illusions of understanding. An experiment that nicely illustrates this is to show people a narrative in which, say, various historical events are played out and various consequences left possible, with roughly equal chances. Reading the narrative cold, this is what experimental subjects conclude. But if they are first told that one particular consequence ensued, they read the narrative as having made this one much more probable than any of the others, stressing whichever bits of the narrative pointed that way and passing over the others. Furthermore, when we know how events turned out, we have highly unreliable memories about how well we predicted them, consistently overestimating our past prophetic powers. Very possibly Tony Blair and George Bush now give themselves full credit for having predicted all along that after their invasion, Iraq would be ungovernable.

A related phenomenon, widely studied and well known to psychologists, is our tendency to cling to beliefs even when any evidence we had for them is explicitly taken away. The famous experiment confirming this involved fake suicide notes, with the subjects of the experiment divided into two groups. Each person was asked if they could distinguish fake from real suicide notes (none of the notes were real), and those in one group were told they had done well on this, and those in the other group told the reverse. Afterward, the subjects were debriefed and told that the results were meaningless. Finally, they were asked to fill in a questionnaire on which they estimated how well they expected to do on any future occasion of detecting genuine suicide notes. Sure enough, those who had "scored" highly predicted they would do better than those who had "scored" badly.

This might seem to be another confirmation of our hair-trigger vanity. But interestingly, the same effect can be obtained with third-party judgments. That is, when people watched the same experiment with stooges performing the same task, and were debriefed in the same way, they nevertheless predicted that the stooges who had been "marked" highly would be better at distinguishing real suicide notes in a future real situation. So it was not just self-love that made the debriefing so ineffectual but the astonishingly sticky nature of ideas. Once one has an idea in one's head, it is profoundly difficult to get rid of it, however decisively it has been exploded.

It is natural to call this tendency irrational and judged purely in terms of aligning our thoughts with the truth, it is so. On the other hand, it may well be adaptive in its own way. Being able to regard some question as closed frees up computational resources. It is a cost to have to keep an open mind, and the stickiness of once-formed opinion is a way of diminishing that cost. We do not revisit everything from the ground up but, fallibly and distortedly perhaps, start from where we take ourselves to have arrived. It is only when we confront the more bizarre consequences of this habit that we become aware of its potential for protecting delusions.

Earlier I quoted Iris Murdoch, who suggested that provided we can stop the vile self from intruding into the way we think about things, the resulting clarity of vision will make for love and truth. Unfortunately, the results we have been considering suggest that her diagnosis must be wrong. Other forces can prevent her desirable outcomes. Our vision may be blurred and our minds addled by past influences, regardless of whether we think in terms of ourselves or not. Just the ghost of a once-held belief may be enough to distort our interpretations and expectations, and the once-held belief need not even have concerned ourselves. But it becomes precious by being our own belief. Other things become precious when they are our own. People are typically unwilling to sell a lottery ticket for what they paid for it; the ticket has become more precious simply by being their very own. They have invested in it, and they are invested in it. Beliefs are like this but worse, since in abandoning a belief we must confess to having been mistaken, whereas in selling a lottery ticket, there is no question of fault. This is why processes of argument and reasoning so seldom succeed in changing anyone's mind.

I now turn from self-esteem and self-confidence to a more conscious concern for ourselves. The first acute and extended moral and philosophical analysis of this was offered by the French philosopher Jean-Jacques Rousseau. He himself was exquisitely sensitive to the opinion of others, believed himself subject to slights of all kinds, and constantly teetered on the edge of full-blown paranoia. He had an excuse, since the France of his day was dominated by the royal court, and, as Smith so wisely said:

> In the courts of princes, in the drawing-rooms of the great, where success and preferment depend, not upon the esteem of intelligent and well-informed equals, but upon the fanciful and foolish favour of ignorant, and proud superiors; flattery and falsehood too often prevail

> over merit and abilities. In such societies the abilities to please are more regarded than the abilities to serve.[3]

Among other things, Rousseau suffered from the bitterest sense of injustice at his treatment by the establishment of church and state. He wrote that "it is true that in France Socrates would not have drunk the hemlock, but he would have drunk a potion infinitely more bitter, of insult, mockery, and contempt a hundred times worse than death."[4] So his writings can be read partly as a self-exorcism, a desire to overcome weaknesses, which he not only saw all around him but also felt in himself. His treatise *Émile* is an extended analysis of what has to be avoided, couched as an educational tract on how to bring up a young man to be free of all the vices and deficiencies that Rousseau saw as a canker in himself and others.

The distinction that structures his work is that between "amour de soi" and "amour propre." The former is honest self-interest, issuing in our desire for basic well-being: health, food, shelter, and security. There is nothing regrettable about that, nor about our attempts to turn material circumstances toward ensuring such things (in Milton's version of paradise, Adam and Eve have to do a good deal of gardening, even before the Fall, while at the end of Voltaire's novel, Candide and his friends retreat from the horrors of the world into their own garden). Indeed, the early part of Émile's education is to give him a useful trade, ensuring his ability to meet his needs in sturdy independence. But amour de soi is easily satisfied. It requires little of the world.

Amour propre is a different, more dangerous, and much hungrier beast. It is essentially comparative and relational. It concerns a person's perception of his or her standing in relation to others.

(Although Rousseau has, as it were, commandeered the idea of amour propre, there were, of course, anticipations. Montaigne, for example, had said that "whatever it is, art or nature, that imprints in us this disposition to live with reference to others, it does us much more harm than good . . . we do not care so much what we are in ourselves and in reality as what we are in the public mind."[5])

So, whereas someone's ordinary self-interest can be forwarded or frustrated, their amour propre is essentially something that can be gratified or offended, bruised or wounded. It refers to our sensitivity to social standing and comparison. At its worst, it acts like a voice in our ear telling us that we have a *right* to take our place in front of others, or a right to their deference and humility. If these are not forthcoming, it poisons us with envy and resentment, and even at or near its best, it brings on greed, competition, and the desire for superiority. It may not be wholly bad, for as we shall shortly see, comparison with others is involved with our potential for pride and shame, and even Rousseau never argues that we should be blithely insensitive to our relations to others. But he does think that amour propre gets out of hand, and he devotes large parts of *Émile* to making sure that in his ideal pupil, it should not do so.

Émile is the ideal male pupil, but we should digress for a moment to consider his female counterpart, Sophy. In a notorious paragraph Rousseau sums up the essential difference between the status, or nature, of men in society and that of women:

> Worth alone will not suffice, a woman must be thought worthy; nor beauty, she must be admired; nor virtue, she must be respected. A woman's honour does not depend on her conduct alone, but on her

> reputation, and no woman who permits herself to be considered vile is really virtuous. A man has no one but himself to consider and so long as he does right he may defy public opinion; but when a woman does right her task is only half finished, and what people think of her matters as much as what she really is. Hence her education must, in this respect be different from man's education. "What people will think" is the grave of a man's virtue and the throne of a woman's.[6]

Insofar as Rousseau was simply reporting on the conventional ethics of his time, this may be unexceptionable, even if the implications of that ethics are regrettable. But he also thought there was something inevitable about it, deriving (as Hume also thought) from the asymmetric roles of men and women in relation to their offspring. And if he were right, it might be thought that I was whistling in the wind earlier when I was careful to suggest that the vanity to which L'Oréal appeals can be discussed in a gender-neutral way. However, I see no reason to doubt that any gender-related asymmetries in the vanities of men and women are the result of culture: nurture, not nature.[7] Be that as it may, it is important to note that Rousseau's deference to the status quo in his world is not, as it stands, a defense of amour propre in women. For they are not being invited to compare themselves with others but only to present a good face to the world; it is not superiority that they are to worry about, but reputation. In principle, the distinction is clear enough, although in practice it may falter, since Rousseau says that admiration is a component of this reputation, and admiration is usually implicitly comparative. Most human traits excite admiration only when they come in a more or less extraordinary degree, in which case poor Sophy is more or less bound to have her quota of amour propre. And this in turn might lead us to query whether Rousseau has set himself a sensible target in the first place. Perhaps odious comparison is part of the human lot, and especially the female lot. I think this reservation must be noted but does not undermine the general thrust.

For Rousseau the principal element that opposes inflamed amour propre is compassion. Again echoing many other moralists before and since, Rousseau hymns the fundamental role of pity and fellow-feeling. He believes it is the first relation to others that touches the human heart, a natural emotion that takes us beyond ourselves so that "we identify with the suffering animal, by leaving, so to speak, our own nature and taking his." Rousseau argues that to develop compassion we must ensure that we regard other people as much like ourselves, and see ourselves as vulnerable to whatever misfortunes strike others. This is an exercise of the imagination. Pity, says ancient wisdom, requires knowing that we may suffer in the same way ourselves. Arrogance, by contrast, shuts off compassion. So, for instance, the banker cannot conceive of earning less than millions, and so is indifferent to the fate of those whom he makes into beggars. The thought that "there but for the grace of God go I" is lost upon him. *Non ignara mali, miseris succurrere disco*—not unacquainted with misfortune, I am learning to help those who are miserable.[8] Rousseau said, "I know nothing so fine, so full of meaning, so touching, so true, as these words."[9] An obvious problem with late capitalist society in England and the United States especially, is that those who are catapulted from wealthy backgrounds to jobs in banks, commercial law, politics, and so forth are very much *ignara mali*. They cannot actually comprehend the position of the others.

The aspects of human nature that shut us off from compassion are above all envy, jealousy, and vanity:

> We must develop that heart and open its doors to his fellow-creatures, and there must be as little self-interest as possible mixed up with these impulses; above all, no vanity, no emulation, no boasting, none of those sentiments which force us to compare ourselves with others; for such comparisons are never made without arousing some measure of hatred against those who dispute our claim to the first place, were it only in our own estimation.[10]

In Rousseau's picture, much human unhappiness and many of the ills of society derive from the insatiable desires that are inflamed simply by comparison with others. Insatiable, because the kind of invidious distinction at which we aim will seldom be satisfied, and for the majority of people can never be satisfied. Even if one day the mirror on the wall tells us that we are the fairest of them all, still we are uneasy, for at any moment it may reveal someone else to have overtaken us, and as in the fairy tale, this engenders malice and hatred, destroying whatever precarious happiness was built upon the imagined sense of preeminence. Human relationships become structured around envy and spite from below, arrogance and contempt from above.

There is nothing enviable about envy. It is a canker, and a shameful one at that. Smith writes that

> as we are always ashamed of our own envy, we often pretend, and sometimes really wish to sympathize with the joy of others, when by that disagreeable sentiment we are disqualified from doing so. We are

> glad, we say on account of our neighbour's good fortune, when in our hearts, perhaps, we are really sorry.[11]

Hypocrisy is here the tribute that vice pays to virtue. We might try a kind of defense, for although envy involves discontent, which is clearly unpleasant, it also has a kind of moral component.[12] It is a reaction to a felt inferiority, but particularly to the idea that the superiority of another is undeserved. It is this that especially galls us, so that envy is more than the wish to occupy the state of another but contains an element of perceived unfairness, and it is this that eats us up, bringing the discontent and malice that belong to it.

We might then think that it is not such a bad thing that we should be on the lookout for unfairness or injustice in the relative situations of persons, so that even if the emotion is self-centered, in that we only feel envy when it is our own worse situation that concerns us, nevertheless, there is a moral concern that is not wholly regrettable. Unfortunately, this glimmer of light is very dim. Envious people do not seem to translate their private emotion into a public, impartial concern for desert and justice. It is their own take on their own relative situation that bothers them, even to the point where it poisons their lives. And we cannot look to envious people for particularly well-tuned senses of injustice. Perhaps there was nothing unjust or undeserved about it at all. Perhaps the better person won, having worked harder and sacrificed more, but envy can still simmer in the breast of the loser. It is very easy to translate the fact that one wanted something into the thought that one deserves it (this is one manifestation of inflamed self-esteem), and thence into the thought that anyone else, who has it when one does not, is a fit object of resentment. A similar dynamic results in our hating those to whom we have behaved badly, thereby excusing our own behavior in our own eyes, a syndrome we already met in the man of hubris, but not unique to him. At any rate, it is a sufficiently common syndrome for Somerset Maugham to comment ironically on its alleged absence in one of his characters:

> Most of us when we have done a caddish thing harbour resentment against the person we have done it to, but Roy's heart, always in the right place, never permitted him such pettiness. He could use a man very shabbily without afterwards bearing him the slightest ill-will.[13]

Maugham is right to imply that Roy is unusual. La Rochefoucauld said that "we can forgive those who bore us, but we cannot forgive those whom we bore." It is as if we need to tell ourselves a self-justifying story so that we were not at fault after all. The upside of this is that if we do someone a good turn, we are more likely to think well of them, and do them another. So a recipe for getting someone to help you twice is to get them to help you once.

Hence, as well, the all-too-human pleasure of Schadenfreude, or mild elation at the (small) misfortune of another. Reading that this celebrity has had to replace an overweight breast implant, or that this other one's toupee blew off at the airport, gives an undeniable frisson of pleasure. This too has a moral component, as if justice is after all reasserting itself. They deserve it that a little rain should fall into their charmed lives, or so we think. If they suffer a real catastrophe, perhaps losing a limb in a car accident, for instance, then in normal people there is no pleasure: nobody deserves to suffer that. We find it amusing if someone superior slips on a banana skin, but not if they fall under a bus. A bad review is a relatively small misfortune, and if a colleague complains of a bad review, our sympathy is all too likely to be mixed with the half-suppressed thought that, well, it was not too surprising, really, rather amusing—he does rather cut corners—whereas when we ourselves get a bad review, an abyss opens in front of us, the frame of the universe is shaken, and the very heavens cry out for justice.

This example may remind us that from the earliest times, philosophers have been aware that we are typically envious of those with whom we most easily compare ourselves and with whom we compete: "potter is furious with potter and craftsman with craftsman, and beggar is envious of beggar and singer of singer."[14] This is usually explained in the case of envy by the fact that in our imaginations we put ourselves in the other's place, and it is easier to imagine being in the place of those close to us than those far away from us, on whatever scale of comparison we are using. In the case of Schadenfreude, it is easy to imagine ourselves in our colleague's place, and to appreciate the mortification they must be feeling, yet any compassion we may therefore feel seems not to diminish the tincture of pleasure. Or perhaps it does diminish it for a moment, if our imagination is sufficiently vivid. Alas, though, and shamefully, it may still return, and we may feel doubly corrupt, albeit quite pleasurably, if we find that the very thought that we should not be amused or elated actually increases our amusement or elation: the cycle that often engenders uncontrollable giggling among children.

The closeness of what is imagined also chimes in with the well-known result of much research on happiness, which suggests a very widespread tendency to think that just an extra 15 percent would make all the difference to one's life, and this wherever on the economic graph one happens to be. One can so easily imagine the arrival of that extra 15 percent, and the joy that the little differences would provide. The reverse effect also exists: if we just miss a train—a bad traffic light, a slow ticket clerk—we are much more annoyed than if we missed it by a mile.[15] Again, however, research also suggests that when people gain their extra 15 percent, while it makes a difference for a while, their level of happiness rapidly returns pretty much to where it was before. The joy is fleeting. In fact, happiness is the response to a *change* rather than a continuous measure of an absolute level at which we are sited. Spinoza emphasized this: "we live in a state of perpetual variation, and, according as we are changed for the better or the worse, we are called happy or unhappy."[16] A letter from the tax authorities, demanding a barely noticeable sum, can plunge the rich recipient into gloom for a day; a day at the races winning, another barely noticeable sum brings a burst of elation. Many people spend some of their happiest days climbing cold, uncomfortable, rather fearful mountains because doing so gives a continuous drip of hard tasks executed and ground grimly gained.

This is one reason why there is a "paradox of hedonism" that can be put in terms of either happiness or pleasure. It is the thought that the least efficient way of finding either happiness or pleasure is to pursue them. Put in terms of happiness, we can see it like this: To be happy you must quite literally "lose yourself." You must lose yourself in some pursuit; you need to forget your own happiness and find other goals and projects, other objects of concern that might include the welfare of some other people, or the cure of the disease, or simply in the variety of everyday activities with their little successes and setbacks. When Apollo pursues Daphne, he will be made happier by closing the gap, more miserable as it opens up. The happiness comes or goes because he has an independent measure of success. And so it is if we pursue some independent goal ourselves. I try to climb a mountain or to pursue philosophical understanding, and am made happy insofar as I perceive progress in that direction, miserable insofar as I feel the reverse. But if I have no independent goal, but simply try to pursue happiness itself, what is the measure of acceleration or deceleration? Sitting around is not accelerating one toward anything, except perhaps the grave. Indolence is a happy state after sufficient activity, but rapidly cloys, so that without a new goal boredom sets in and, according to Schopenhauer, is the next worse thing to pain: "If, over and above freedom from pain, there is also an absence of boredom, the essential conditions of earthly happiness are attained; for all else is chimerical." We might be reminded of the desolation of Maria von Herbert, touched upon earlier.

The pursuit of happiness rapidly turns into the pursuit of wealth, which soon becomes a vast, limitless end in itself. To introduce this topic, it is good to have a term from zoology at hand. Seagoing birds that dive for fish, such as the gannets of the Hebrides or the boobies of the Galapagos Islands, provide one of nature's most wonderful spectacles. Circling at a great height, they spot fish underwater and launch themselves downward at extraordinary speed, cleaving the water like javelins before coming up triumphantly with their prey. Unfortunately, other birds await them. The great skua or bonxie will attack and harass the gannet until it disgorges its meal, which the skua then makes off with; frigate birds do the same to boobies.

Zoologists call this way of living kleptoparasitism. It is found among human beings as well, and it is only too easy to select representative statistics out of the huge number that document its recent ascendancy. Here is a recent description of changes in the US economy:

> The path that the division of corporate value added has taken since 1980 is reflected in data on productivity, pay, and income shares. From 1947 to 1979, productivity rose 119%, average compensation of production and non-supervisory workers (who constitute more than four-fifths of the private-sector labor force) grew 100%, and the share of national income received by the top 1 percent of earners (which would include most of top corporate management) ranged from 9 to 13%. From 1979 to 2009, in contrast productivity rose 80%, worker compensation rose 8%, and the top 1 percent of earners increased their share of national income to more than 23%.[17]

In fact, the very, very rich, the top .1 percent of Americans, take more than 12 percent of America's pretax income. Greed is good; there is no such thing as society; and the only duty a company owes is to its owners. Since few people born since 1980 or so will be familiar with the extraordinary change in the philosophical climate that happened then, or can even imagine that once the moral climate was entirely different, it is important to stress that this is actually a very recent creed. In 1981 the American Business Roundtable could still claim that "corporations have a responsibility, first of all, to make available to the public quality goods and services at fair prices . . . the long-term viability of a corporation depends upon its responsibility to the society of which it is a part." How quaint! By 1997 the same organization proclaimed that "the principal objective of a business enterprise is to generate economic returns to its owners . . . ."[18]

Thatcher, Reagan, and Milton Friedman had taken over, and their absolute command of the spirit of the age continues, in spite of the visible damage to their people. To continue, 1 percent of Americans own 30 percent of the country's personal wealth; the funds of the wealthiest three people in America would pay off the total deficit of all the States of the Union. Four hundred people control the same amount of wealth as the poorer half of the nation. To put this last figure in perspective: each of those 400 has wealth equivalent to that of nearly 400,000 fellow citizens: enough to fill five of the largest football stadiums. Talk of a social contract, in the face of these figures, sounds like what it is—a hollow mockery.

With the rare exceptions of the happiest countries in the world (especially the Scandinavians), inequality has accelerated worldwide for the last forty years, since the lurch to the right in the last decades of the twentieth century. But we can compare a different figure: directors of the top 500 British companies awarded themselves on average a 49 percent pay rise in 2010–11, a year in which the economy stagnated and the rest of the population saw their incomes fall substantially. In the United States, with the same stagnant economy, CEOs were uncharacteristically restrained, and contented themselves with a 40 percent rise. In the United States during the first two years of the faltering recovery of 2009 to 2011, average family income grew by a modest 1.7 percent, "but the gains were very uneven. Top 1 percent incomes grew by 11.2 percent while bottom 99 percent incomes shrunk by 0.4 percent."[19] It becomes a habit: according to a report on National Public Radio, in 2012 the wealth of the top 1 percent again increased by 20 percent, while that of the average worker increased by only 1 percent.

The horrified reaction of anyone with a tincture of civic sense is to ask how they can do it? How can they look themselves in the mirror, walk down the street? Have they no sense of decency, let alone fellow-feeling with the rest, whom they have robbed and continue to rob? Are they no better than the kleptocracies of the third world with their paranoid dictators and their grisly apparatus of repression? It is one thing to be a kleptoparasite, but how can anyone be a kleptoparasite without shame? Perhaps they forget to wonder how they appear to others: it is as if, not knowing Hume's dictum that the minds of men are mirrors to one another, they walk around with "stinking breath" but without any self-consciousness about it (see chapter 1).

We have already seen part of the answer in the self-attribution fallacy. Otherwise reasonable people, surrounded by courtiers, need to believe, and therefore find it easy to believe, that they are worth it because of their exceptional abilities, judgment, and intelligence. Anything less than, say, 400 times the average income of workers in their companies would be unjust, a simple failure to reward their astonishing gifts adequately. This belief can grip even reasonable people, but then, we have already talked of the prevalence of psychopathic personality types at the top of the business heap, so very often these are not reasonable people. A man (it is usually men) on the board of a bank may convince himself that it requires extraordinary genius to offer those who lend money to the bank (customers) 1 percent interest, but only lend to borrowers at 16.5 percent interest, and to pocket as much of the difference as he can get away with.[20]

The fact that any high-school student could do the sums does not seem to impinge on this colossal self-deception. Of course, there are in any industry people of real merit who may command something more than the average. But it is much easier to believe you belong to this class than to do so, and the belief is unlikely to be shaken if the craft skill is, as one banker is supposed to have boasted, "that of playing Russian roulette with other people's heads."

As important as hoarding all the credit to oneself is the inability to comprehend the position of the other 99 percent or even

99.9 percent: secure in their smoke-tinted limousines and gated communities, the kleptoparasites are literally *ignara mali*. As Rousseau went on to say:

> Why have kings no pity on their people? Because they never expect to be ordinary men. Why are the rich so hard on the poor? Because they have no fear of becoming poor. Why do the nobles look down upon the people? Because a nobleman will never be one of the lower classes. . . .

So another aspect of greed is that the fat cats fence themselves off, maintaining as far as possible their ignorance of ill. Sometimes the results would be laughable were they not so harmful. In their book *Unjust Rewards*, Polly Toynbee and David Walker give results of a 2007 survey of the top 1 percent of earners in the City of London. These hugely high-flying executives, lawyers, and bankers had completely fantastical views about the country they lived in and allegedly "ran":

> But if myopia is a common condition, the high earners of Canary Wharf turned out to be as blind as bats. They knew less about earnings than the general public and were less accurate than the top 10% of earners in the BSA survey. Our bankers and lawyers were all comfortably in the top 1% of earners, many in the top 0.1%, yet here they were saying that 6% of earners were better off than them. They earned £150,000 [about $290,000] plus, yet placed themselves on the scale below those actually earning £50,000 [about $98,000] (pre-tax). One even placed himself plum in the middle, imagining 50% earned more than him—when the middle or median earnings, the halfway point at which half of full-time earners in the UK get paid more and half

> less, were £23,764 [about $47,000] pre-tax in April 2007. They wanted to compare themselves with richer people, inventing a society in which they are a step or two down from the top. Comparing themselves upwards not downwards, they considered themselves normal, when they were anything but.
>
> A high income in 2007 was £39,825 [about $78,000], the sum it took to put an earner into the top tax band. Some 90% of the UK's 31.6 million taxpayers earned less than that, a fiscal fact our group found hard to believe. They over-estimated by four times what it takes to enter that top 10% bracket of earners in the UK: they thought it was £162,000 [about $317,000].[21]

Similarly, in the 2012 presidential race, Mitt Romney suggested that a "middle income" family in America would earn about $250,000, whereas in fact the median income for a family of four was just one-quarter of that sum. This might be merely comical, except that it undoubtedly helped all those incredibly brilliant financiers and analysts to grossly misvalue everything else in their hands, precipitating the crisis in 2008 that led to the current recession in the Western world.

One might think that this simply shows that top CEOs, lawyers, bankers, and politicians are ignorant and unimaginative, on top of the other personality disorders we have already described. But of course their imaginations are intact enough in one direction. For there is one kind of person that fully engages the fat cat's imagination: fatter cats. Envy fuels the kleptoparasitic leapfrog, accelerated by transparency requirements that pretty much make earnings public knowledge. Remuneration committees, made up by people either earning comparable amounts to those whose pay they determine or employed by people who themselves do so, and who therefore would not welcome anything that rocked the boat, report that the constant refrain is that the people in some other companies earn more—everyone compares themselves with the top quartile of directors' pay—so that it is actually unjust that I, every bit as deserving as he, should be paid only millions whereas he is paid tens of millions. In case this seems overstated, shed a tear for poor, suffering Prince Alwaleed bin Talal, deemed in 2013 to have a fortune of $20 billion by *Forbes* magazine, who was so upset at not being placed in the world's top ten—but rather merely listed as the richest person in Saudi Arabia—that he has been driven to sue the publisher for defamation. And so it goes, with envy for those above and indifference to those below, vanity, psychopathy, culpable ignorance, self-deception, and lack of imagination all contributing richly to cocktail hour in the City.

In case it is thought unlikely that envy and the corresponding desire to excite envy should motivate these rational, economic men, we might remember the old story about the man who is offered by a fairy any gift he wishes—provided only that his neighbor will also receive twice what he requests. After some thought, he asks to lose one eye.

Perhaps, fortunately, the diminishing marginal utility of money rapidly irons out any advantage in terms of happiness that these astronomical incomes bring about. The difference in ability to live a decent life between a poor Somali woman struggling to feed her dying children and an ordinary middle-class worker who earns, say, $60,000 each year, is incomparably greater than that between the worker's life and the life of the CEO who earns $6,000,000 a year. So one might think that the huge and increasing inequalities are of little real significance. However, after the 2008 collapse, the bank bailouts and continued predations of the rich transferred huge amounts of private debt onto the government books, leaving most governments with little option, as they saw it, than to cut social welfare, thereby pushing as many of their citizens as possible toward the plight of the Somali woman.[22]

The ancient Greeks had another myth, that of Midas, the king of Phrygia or Western Turkey. Although already rich, when he was offered the chance of getting whatever he wished for, the best he could imagine was that everything he touched should turn to gold. This wish was granted, and the result was highly pleasing—for a short while. But it turned into a nightmare as his food turned to gold, and then his daughter when he kissed her. In no time he was begging to be released from the curse, and, unusually for someone with a fatal flaw in Greek dramas, this was eventually granted him. As with the myth of Narcissus, the moral is wider than we might think. It is difficult for rich people to be friends with poor people, and difficult for the very rich to have satisfying human relations with anybody or anything. The worm of fear sees to that. The plutocrat needs a gated community and bodyguards whom he hopes he can trust, but may fear he cannot. His business associates will be out to cheat him, or so he will fear. Any chance of friendship is likely to be poisoned by the fear that the friend is only in it for gain; families themselves are wrecked by envy and bitterness, boredom and desolation, all of which follow on the heels of excess money. Lottery winners tend to have grotesquely distorted lives, where tawdry opulence is paid for by forfeiting any chance of more ordinary, greater pleasures. And yet the spell is hard to break. Few seem able to resist the lure of more, and then more, far beyond the point where the marginal utility curve begins to slope downward.

Perhaps the most horrifying examples of those at the top maintaining willful blindness to the rest arise in military history from the gulf between generals and men. Military historian Basil Liddell Hart says, on the battle of Passchendaele during the 1914–18 war:

> Perhaps the most damning comment on the plan which plunged the British Army in this bath of mud and blood is contained in an incidental revelation of the remorse of one who was largely responsible for it [the chief of staff of the overall commander, General Haig]. This highly placed officer from G.H.Q. was on his *first* visit to the battle front—at the end of four months' battle. Growing increasingly uneasy as the car approached the swamplike edges of the battle area, he eventually burst into tears, crying "Good God did we really send men to fight in that?" To which his companion replied that the ground was far worse ahead. If the exclamation was a credit to his heart it revealed on what a foundation of delusion and inexcusable ignorance his indomitable "offensiveness" had been based.[23]

Here another observation from philosophers has been confirmed by experience with law courts and psychological experiments alike. This is that individual stories and individual experiences matter in a way that generalities do not. The top brass needed to see for themselves.

> In general, it may be affirmed, that there is no such passion in human minds, as the love of mankind, merely as such, independent of personal qualities, of services, or of relation to ourself. It is true, there is no human, and indeed no sensible, creature, whose happiness or misery does not, in some measure, affect us when brought near to us, and represented in lively colours: But this proceeds merely from sympathy, and is no proof of such an universal affection to mankind . . . .[24]

Or, as Joseph Stalin is reported to have said, "One death is a tragedy; one million is a statistic." If nothing rubs your nose in the tragedy of an individual, the economic or social policy that engenders millions of such tragedies fails to engage us either. The famous phrase that provides the measure of value according to utilitarianism, "the greatest happiness of the greatest number" picks out an abstraction of no imaginative substance. It is fine as a label but will not motivate us or upset us in the same way as a close engagement with a single unhappy soul. And by averting his eyes from individuals, the king, rich man, or nobleman can avoid any potential murmurings from his conscience.

A confirmation of this in the law courts is that companies whose doings impact unfavorably on whole towns or populations are fined less in punitive damages than those who affect a very few. The few have faces and stories that can engage the sympathy of judge and jury, but the many do not. There is, however, an upside to this, which is the power of the individual story. As engaged novelists like Dickens or Harriet Beecher Stowe well understood, and as charities show every day, an individual narrative or a single picture of an individual suffering is of more use to the campaigner or reformer than some abstract statistic about social ills or deprivation.

The reverse side of the coin to envy is arrogance or contempt. Here the superior, again in whichever scale is in play, looks down on the position of the inferior and plumes himself on his relative standing. In real life this is probably as ubiquitous as Schadenfreude, but although we know that others feel it, it remains unpardonable for them to express it. The person who lets you understand his sense of superiority, and his pride in his own self and relative contempt of yours, is about as odious as can be. This may seem odd, given that it is the habitual stance of the idol in the advertisement or on the catwalk, as we have already seen. Yet in real company, away from our imaginings in front of the advertising poster, modesty, when we feel ourselves rather better than others, is a virtue when it comes naturally, and a duty if it does not.

The distortions in human affairs caused by greed and envy are all around us. For thirty years or more, and particularly since the triumph of capitalism over the old communist orders, market enthusiasts have preached that greed is good, and that the finest aim in human life is to claw oneself to the top of the riches ladder. But greed is not good. The claim that it is so was originally satirical and put in the mouth of the appalling financial hotshot Gordon Gekko, played by Michael Douglas in the 1987 movie *Wall Street*:

> The point is, ladies and gentleman, that greed, for lack of a better word, is good. Greed is right, greed works. Greed clarifies, cuts through, and captures the essence of the evolutionary spirit. Greed, in all of its forms; greed for life, for money, for love, knowledge has marked the upward surge of mankind.

But it is dangerous to satirize the spirit of the age. Reality has a way of catching up with the satire, and certainly did so in this case. Greed is, as we have described, the inordinate desire for the envy of others, or the desire that others think less well of themselves than they do of you. As Smith said, the other advantages of wealth over decent sufficiency are largely chimerical, but this is the one that fuels the boardroom race.

One of the nicest passages in which an author laments the nature of these passions occurs in the constitutional theory of the second president of the United States, John Adams, who argued that a proper constitution for a country must take account of the infirmities of the people who make it up:

> The passions are all unlimited; nature has left them so: if they could be bounded, they would be extinct; and there is no doubt they are of indispensable importance in the present system. They certainly increase too, by exercise, like the body. The love of gold grows faster than the heap of acquisition: the love of praise increases by every gratification, till it stings like an adder, and bites like a serpent; till the man is miserable every moment when he does not snuff the incense: ambition strengthens at every advance, and at last takes possession of the whole soul so absolutely, that the man sees nothing in the world of importance to others, or himself, but in his object. The subtlety of these three passions, which have been selected from all the others because they are aristocratical passions, in subduing all others, and even the understanding itself, if not the conscience too, until they become absolute and imperious masters of the whole mind, is a curious speculation. The cunning with which they hide themselves from others, and from the man himself too; the patience with which they wait for opportunities; the torments they voluntarily suffer for a time, to secure a full enjoyment at length; the inventions, the discoveries, the contrivances they suggest to the understanding, sometimes in the dullest dunces in the world, if they could be described in writing, would pass for great genius.[25]

Evidently, John Adams would not have been surprised by results like those of Polly Toynbee and David Walker.

It might seem as if the only escape from this treadmill of unhappiness and disappointment would be to live the life of a solitary, alone on a desert island. But Rousseau does not think that: he knows that men have to live among men. The real defense begins, as we have seen, with compassion. But compassion involves an imaginative displacement into the state of another, and it is this imaginative power, more evenly directed, that is the key to a better social world. We have amour propre, in that we do need recognition and respect from other people; we can, after all, be insulted, affronted, demeaned, and humiliated. But a fully developed imagination enables us to appreciate that just as we have our amour propre, so too do other people. It is therefore unreasonable to ask them to give more to you than you give to them. It is an offense against equality and reciprocity. These entail demanding only such recognition and respect from other people as they can justly demand from you. In this dimension, there are no pedestals. In other words, if you ever think "because I am worth it," you must also think, "because every individual is worth it."

6

Respect

The philosopher who made the most of the ideas we have been approaching was Immanuel Kant. Although a very capable astronomer, Kant lived too long ago to know that we live on a tiny planet of one of the millions of stars at the edge of one out of something like one hundred thousand million galaxies. But he did know that human beings "in the system of nature" are simply insignificant, tiny animals scurrying about the surface of an insignificant and tiny planet in an insignificant and tiny part of the cosmos. However, he insisted, this contrasts wholesale with human beings regarded as *persons*. One of Kant's most famous quotations is:

> Two things fill the mind with ever new and increasing admiration and awe, the oftener and more steadily we reflect upon them: the starry heavens above me and the moral law within me. I do not

> merely conjecture them and seek them as though obscured in darkness or in the transcendent region beyond my horizon; I see them before me, and I associate them directly with the consciousness of my existence.[1]

Self-respect is appropriate, in Kant's picture, precisely because each of us has the capacity to recognize, and to obey, the "moral law within." It is our capacity to subject ourselves to principles that separate us from mere wanton, animal existence. It gives us our capacity to resist temptation, and to act as judges capable of weighing—and sometimes rejecting and regretting—our own doings. It is this capacity to deliberate while binding ourselves to a moral law that both gives us our dignity and enforces guilt or shame, the consciousness of having fallen short, when we do things that betray it.

Of course, this raises the question of where this "moral law" comes from, and what its dictates are. Here arise the difficulties that fill the volumes of commentary on Kant's overall moral picture, even if the general direction is clear enough. The easiest version to understand is the so-called formula of humanity: "So act that you use humanity, whether in your own person or in the person of any other, always at the same time as an end, never merely as a means."[2]

This clearly insists on respect for the humanity in other persons, on not treating people as mere means to your own ends, on not acting in ways that you could not accept other people acting. It is most clearly flouted by acts of deception and manipulation. These deny victims the power to use their own reason on the situation. By deceiving a person, an agent prevents the victim from deliberating together with him about the course of action that they are to follow. So perhaps under the guise of friendship and cooperation, the deceiver is bent on manipulating the agent's decision making, or denying their right to assess things as they are and then to make up their own mind. In serious cases this may amount to a betrayal, a fit cause of the resentment that we saw Smith describing above. It is this denial of the humanity of the other that is the crime.

Of course, interpreting the formula is not easy. Does it, for instance, imply a distinction between outright lying, and merely being "economical with the truth"? This is a natural enough distinction, with lying scoring much lower than mere evasion, yet the latter also denies the listener the possibility of a full play of his or her reason on whatever issue is at hand.[3] Yet ruling out this economy with the truth would make many human interactions very difficult. A civilized first date or the early stages of a seduction may essentially depend on a decent indirection, a disguise of any—heaven forbid!—carnal intentions. Barging in with coarse suggestions would precipitate certain failure. Yet one would not want to rule out such social delicacies as morally impermissible. But if this kind of disguise or misdirection is sometimes acceptable, how could it be that outright lying, which in many cases is less likely to work as the agent wishes, is so much worse?

The first formulation of the categorical imperative speaks not of respecting the humanity of another, or of respecting oneself, but of whether you could intend the principle or "maxim" of your action to be one that everyone follows. The formula of universal law commands: "Act only in accordance with that maxim through which you can at the same time will that it become a universal law."[4] This is, of course, reminiscent of the familiar "golden rule" of doing to others what you would have them do to you. It also bears some relationship to Rousseau's idea that you should demand as much respect from others as you are prepared to offer them. But it goes beyond this, for if you think we live in a dog-eat-dog world, you might happily snarl at others when you are able to do so, accepting that this is what you would expect them to do to you were the positions reversed. Whereas Kant wants the law to encompass universal respect, not mutual hostility.[5]

We need not take on the difficult tasks of interpretation and exposition that Kant left behind. What is important for our concern is that it is simply this ability to conform our will to the categorical imperative, in its clothing either as the formula of humanity or as the formula of universal law, that gives us real worth, real value, or real dignity. However small and insignificant we may feel ourselves to be in the scale of the universe of all space and all time, in our ordinary human perspective, things are otherwise. We are to deal with each other, and to be dealt with, as persons:

> But a human being regarded as a *person*, that is, as the subject of a morally practical reason, is exalted above any price, for as a person he is not to be valued merely as a means to the ends of others or even to his own ends, but as an end in himself, that is, he possesses a *dignity* (an absolute inner worth) by which he exacts *respect* for himself from all other rational beings in the world. He can measure himself with every other being of this kind and value himself on a footing of equality with them.
>
> Humanity in his person is the object of the respect which he can demand from every other human being, but which he must also not forfeit . . . his insignificance as a *human animal* may not infringe upon his consciousness of his dignity as a *rational human being*, and he

> should not disavow the moral self-esteem of such a being . . . and this self-esteem is a duty of man to himself.[6]

Kant was no Pollyanna: he thought that human beings could be contemptible enough. But properly to judge someone contemptible would not be to compare them unfavorably to oneself or anyone else but to judge their behavior by "the moral law within" and to find it falling short. And then, although the individual might be contemptible, the "humanity in him" is not, but remains the object of respect or reverence. Whether we can manage so cleanly to separate the contemptible individual from the respectable humanity within him might trouble us, but Kant suggests that if we try we can manage it.

This self-respect is at the same time an inescapable facet of our natures, but also gives us a kind of command to respect ourselves and others equally. Treating our own rational agency as a pearl beyond price, we are, Kant supposes, forced to admit that the pearl beyond price is also found in the rational agency of everyone, wherever it is found. We offend against the respect owed to other people if we treat them as "mere means" to our own ends, or put them in servile or dominated positions. But we equally offend against it if we are ourselves servile or unduly humble, or if we submit to the domination of others. As a result, Kant was a good deal more wary than Iris Murdoch about the supposed virtue of humility:

> Humility in comparing oneself with other human beings (and indeed with any finite being, even a seraph) is no duty; rather, trying to equal or surpass others in this respect, believing that in this way one will get an even greater inner worth is *ambition*, which is directly

> contrary to one's duty to others. But belittling one's own moral worth merely as a means to acquiring the favor of another, whatever it may be (hypocrisy and flattery) is false (lying) humility, which is contrary to one's duty to oneself since it degrades one's personality.[7]

And he pithily sums it up: "One who makes himself a worm cannot complain afterwards if people step on him." Of course, humiliating oneself may be a kind of aggression: a tactic to shame some other party into doing what one wants, and hence also a kind of manipulation of the other party. The odious Uriah Heep in *David Copperfield*, displaying his humility like a sore, but eaten up inside by venom and envy, is a good example of this association. In other cultures it is actually a part of the repertoire. So in India a "sitting protest" or hunger strike on his doorstep is a way of shaming a creditor into forgiving a debt; Gandhi later exploited the psychology of this brilliantly in order to shame the Raj into conceding political power to Indians themselves. In the Northern Ireland Maze prison, a similar tactic ("dirty protests") was brought to bear to force the British government not to regard IRA dissidents as ordinary criminals or murderers.[8] It is at the least profoundly embarrassing to see some fellow human deliberately abasing themselves, and if you have it in your power to raise them up, you may feel an internal sanction from that discomfort, or may fear an external sanction from the bad opinion of other people, compelling you to do it.

It is because of this self-respect that we have duties to ourselves as well as others, and Kant thought many other duties derived from this. So, for instance, a propensity to wanton destruction of parts of nature is opposed to a human being's duty to himself, since it "weakens or uproots" a disposition that we ought to value, namely, the disposition to love things for themselves even apart from any intention of using them.[9] Similarly, we have duties to animals, since cruelty or neglect would dull a person's feeling for their suffering, and so weaken or uproot a disposition that is "very serviceable to morality in one's relations with other men."

As for the source of the law, Kant is often interpreted as thinking that as rational agents, we prescribe it to ourselves. It is not imposed on us from "outside," for instance, as a kind of reflection of the demands of a vigilant God, or as the demands made on us by one another, or by society as a whole, or even a remainder from the discipline imposed on us by parents in childhood. It is our own self-imposition. But this is a very difficult notion to understand, for how can I, as legislator, bind myself as subject to legislation? If one day I bind myself, say, not to walk on cracks in the pavement, then there is nothing to prevent me from repealing the rule the following day. I can make resolutions, sure enough, but I can also break them, and quite often the breaking is just as sensible as the original intention. I may disappoint myself—or perhaps I just came to my senses and realized I was following a stupid fetish of my own making. Yet we cannot escape our real duties and obligations so easily. So perhaps it is better to say not that we prescribe the law to ourselves but that we come across it within ourselves. It is, after all, very difficult to look someone in the eye, to remain on all fours with them, to expect friendship and cooperation, if we have been caught using them as a "mere means," treading on the respect owed to them and therefore knowing ourselves to be a fit object for their resentment. The categorical imperative is to be inescapable, not adjustable whenever it is convenient to ignore it.

In historical fact, the idea of ourselves being the source of our own laws, instead of reason within us being that source, marks a shift away from Kant. It marks the revolt against universal, impersonal reason toward the valorization of the deepest springs of the self, and this is, in fact, exactly the Romantic revolution against the Enlightenment. It is in the Romantic imagination that the moral hero is one who acts from the deepest wellsprings in his own being, the inner individual kernel to which he is true at all costs. We discuss this further in chapter 7, but remembering that this is a huge shift away from Kant reminds us how difficult it is to find a stable Kantian account of the sources of the moral law.

Kant might have done better to take a leaf out of Smith's book, or anticipate Collingwood's later insight, and accept the fact that our sense of duty, respect, right, and wrong is not the result of pure self-will but is borne in upon us by social training, the signs of affection and aversion other people give us, the stories and examples we are told about in childhood, and the endless smiles and frowns that greet our conduct when we enter into the social world. It has been estimated that parents (or at least parents unsullied by the self-esteem industry) correct their young children on the average of once every eight minutes of their waking lives, so it is not so surprising that the voice of criticism eventually becomes internalized, inexorable, and perhaps fearful. The boundary between falling short in other people's eyes and falling short in our own eyes becomes blurred and permeable. As we said at the end of chapter 2, other people can by threats or incentives create in us a conscience that—and this is the amazing bit—can then operate in successful opposition to threats and incentives.

The essential point for the present is that Kant is offering a bipartite theory of human motivation. On the one hand there are things that he would put under the heading of "inclinations": such things as desires, appetites, sentiments, and feelings. On the other hand, there is the moral law, which itself is somehow not the creature of these contingent and variable factors in our minds but the universal birthright of any rational person. Desires and appetites are all very well when they are directed in the right way, which is why Kant talked above of dispositions such as compassion being "serviceable to morality."[10] Serviceable, but apparently not the real thing. The real thing only comes when you act out of a sense of duty or a sense of rectitude—out of respect for the law.

It is this rather chilly feature of Kant's position that prompted his contemporary Friedrich Schiller's famous jibe: "I serve my friends gladly, but alas I do it with pleasure, hence I am plagued with doubt that I am not virtuous," to which he imagines the Kantian reply: "there is no other advice, you must try to despise them so you may dislike doing what duty commands you to do." This is certainly unfair to Kant (neither does it represent Schiller's own highly Kantian view of ethics; it more likely represents Schiller's caricature of unfair objections to Kant) both because in Kant you can want to do something, or enjoy doing it, even if it is also your duty, and also because, at least in his more humane writings, it seems that you can score some marks in the dimension of virtue for having benevolent and compassionate inclinations, so that you do not have to think of yourself as acting from principle as you do helpful or generous things for family, friends, or the needy in general. All Kant is really doing is asking whether you would still have performed some duty had you had no other inclination to do it. The answer to this question is finally decisive when it is a question of how much you are acting as a person of *principle*, which is the measure of your strength of moral character.

So Kant puts humanity on a pedestal because of our capacity for this genuinely principled self-government. This is more than self-control, although it implies it. It is more because we can exercise self-control in other, lesser ways than by mobilizing respect for any moral law. It might take a good deal of self-control to be properly servile, for instance. Wanting to curry favor with the boss, I need to control the temptation to laugh at his idiotic suggestions or to blow raspberries at his daft ideas. Here I would exercise self-control by taking a particular view of my own self-interest and then scheming to advance it partly by resisting various temptations. This would not be acting morally in Kant's sense. This is strategic self-control, but it is only self-control in the name of principle that propels us up the moral scoreboard.

Kant is dancing on a very high wire, and philosophers divide over whether he falls off it. But the widely agreed nugget of truth in his position is the value of self-respect, and its essential role in enabling us to respect others. A person who lacks self-respect regarding himself, let us say, with self-loathing, as a miserable, shameful, disgusting worm, lacks any kind of springboard from which to think better of others. A slave himself, he sees others as likewise slavish. He is on the road to cynicism, since despairing of good behavior from himself, he will despair of it from others (and he may have reason, for it may have been the hostilities of a cruel world that brought him to this plight). He is to be pitied, but far from admired.

And this brings us back to the other pivotal notion in the emotions of self-reference: pride. Proper pride is quite distinct from hauteur and vanity with their unlovely associations with greed and envy, although it certainly contains some reference to the potential for the admiration of other people. As a first approximation, we might think that pride is a pleasurable anticipation of this admiration, a kind of anticipatory basking in the imagined praise or envy of other people. Typically, we will be prone to feel this pleasure when we select something about ourselves and admire ourselves for it. The emotion can then be appropriate if what we have selected indeed deserves admiration—say, a particular achievement or success in something difficult. It would be a very dour moralist who forbade us from taking pleasure in doing things well.

Pride also contains the possibility of discounting actual admiration. If I have executed a piece of work badly, but well enough to get past a gullible public, I should not feel pride about it but secret embarrassment or even shame.[11] The philosopher G. E. Moore's wife told how when he was about to deliver one of his best-known papers to the Aristotelian Society, Moore was full of anxiety and misgivings. "Don't worry," said his wife, "I am sure they will love it." "Well, they shouldn't," replied the morose Moore. Pride contains a "normative" or evaluative dimension: we feel it when we think we *deserve* the admiration of others, not merely when we *anticipate* it. And properly speaking, anticipation is not necessary, for we may be silently proud of something we did well but in secret, such as a quiet act of anonymous charity, so that we are not anticipating actual applause at all (although we may in some sense be imagining it). And the admiration of others is not sufficient, since unmerited applause ought to be embarrassing rather than pleasurable, even if it must be admitted that our ability to succumb to the pleasure of undeserved basking has a well-known place among human infirmities. We are not all as good as Moore.

If Christian thought were right in placing pride as the root of all evil, this imaginative rehearsal of the deserved admiration of other people would seem to be a Bad Thing. Yet on the face of it, the case is quite different. First, there is an undoubtedly good component in it: thinking we deserve or do not deserve admiration is an exercise of self-evaluation, a willingness to apply standards to which one subscribes to one's own conduct and assess it in their light. In order to feel proud of his work, an artist, for example, has to have thought in terms of achievement, potential failure, something done better when it could easily have been done worse. The possibility of pride therefore depends on the situation. I cannot feel proud of walking down the street, since it is a normal activity well within my normal capacities. But were I recovering from some serious, paralyzing accident or illness, I might feel proud of it, while I myself might feel proud of climbing a hefty mountain, although a professional fell runner would regard it as lightly as I regard the walk down the street, and be thoroughly ashamed at only managing my maximum pace. Our standards of achievement properly vary. Pride involves submitting our own conduct or our own work to criticism, and thankfully coming out intact. Pride would here consort with a sense of relief that any of a number of pitfalls have been avoided. And second, the imagined voice of others is a powerful reality check. Inability to see ourselves as others see us is not so much the mark of a happy innocent as a potential dissociation from the social world, and from the possibility of deploying any sense of one's own merit or demerit at all.

As we have described, people can be proud not so much of things that deserve admiration but merely of things that may get it. And since we are at best fallen angels, these may include all kinds of features that should not reflect particularly well on the subject. A person may be proud of his birth, proud of an accident (proud of having won the lottery, for instance), or proud of the doings of a member of his or her family, tribe, football team, or nation. Provided it is possible to identify oneself with a group, one may be proud of the alleged merits of the group. And, of course, too much pride breeds all kinds of problems, as the Christian moralists were right to notice. Arrogance, ambition, insensitivity to others, and dismissal of the good luck or accidents that helped one along are among the less attractive hangers-on that surround any just, but pleasurable, awareness of things that are genuinely good about oneself. But the real fly in the ointment, to the Christian, is the association of pride with the absence of submission, with disobedience, and eventually rebellion. These associations are significant enough to occupy us in much more detail in chapter 7, but it has to be firmly borne in mind that they are associated with particular exercises or manifestations of pride rather than with each and every occasion of it. The young child proud of his or her piano performance is not thereby chafing at restraint, nor anywhere near the territory of disobedience. They may only be so skilled because they are naturally obedient to teachers and parents, after all.

In *The Nicomachean Ethics*, Aristotle describes his paradigm admirable character, the "magnanimous" or "great-souled" man.

> The magnanimous man, then, seems to be the one who thinks himself worthy of great things and is really worthy of them . . . the magnanimous person, then, is at the extreme in so far as he makes great claims. But in so far as he makes them rightly, he is intermediate; for what he thinks he is worthy of reflects his real worth, while the others are excessive or deficient . . . he has one concern above all. Worth is said to make one worthy of external goods; and we would suppose that the greatest of these is the one we award to the gods, the one above all that is the aim of people with a reputation for worth, the prize for the finest achievements. All this is true of honour, since it is called the greatest of the external goods.

Aristotle goes on to explain that the magnanimous person will be virtuous, and

> Magnanimity then looks like a sort of adornment of the virtues; for it makes them greater, and does not arise without them . . . when he receives great honours from excellent people, he will be moderately pleased, thinking he is getting what is proper to him, or even less. For there can be no honour worthy of complete virtue; but still he will accept excellent people's honours, since they have nothing greater to award him.

The list continues. The magnanimous person will accept honors only from the great, but disdain those from lesser mortals; he will count power and riches for little, although he will count them for something, and as a result might appear arrogant. He is no lover of dangers but "faces them in a great cause, and whenever he faces them he is unsparing of his life, since he does not think life at all costs is worthwhile." He confers benefits but is ashamed of receiving them. He is inactive and lethargic except for some great honor or achievement. He is open and straightforward, since concealment and evasion are the devices of frightened persons, and he is free from fear. He is subordinate to nobody, and cannot let anyone else, except a friend, determine his life's course. He does not gossip; he does not care about small things; and finally, Aristotle tells us gravely, he has slow movements, a deep voice, and calm speech "for since he takes few things seriously, he is in no hurry, and since he counts nothing great, he is not strident."[12]

He sounds like a pompous ass. Aristotle says that someone who falls short of this ideal on one side is unduly humble, and someone who exceeds it on the other side is unduly vain. Commenting on this description, Russell remarked waspishly "one shudders to think what a vain man would be like."[13] It is indeed easy for us to read it as near to a parody, describing some monster of self-esteem or self-deification. But we should look a little more closely.

Aristotle is clearly describing someone at the top of the heap in a society in which there are hierarchies of status and honor. So we have trouble transcribing it into our own more egalitarian and more democratic world. Indeed, the very translation of Aristotle's term for this character gives trouble. The Oxford translation by W. D. Ross has "pride" for "magnanimous." Neither word is quite right. Aristotle is in fact aiming to describe a "proper nobility" of character, but the word "noble" does not figure much in contemporary language, or contemporary society.

If we do transcribe this ideal into our world, what might remain? Perhaps more than we might expect. First, the ideal requires genuine virtue. It also requires an awareness of that virtue, or a degree of self-consciousness. And this in turn requires an awareness of virtue in others, which implies a true assessment of human life and the capacities necessary to make it go well. Those of a skeptical or relativistic bent might raise an eyebrow at the word "true" here, pointing out that there are various views about what makes life go well, and then asking, who is to say which is better than another? Aristotle's own biologically inspired answer makes the analogy between virtue and health, supposing that there is but one healthy way for human beings to live, just as there is but one way for a rose or daffodil to flourish. We may find this analogy strained, since it is more obviously true that there are different ways for a human being to flourish. Cultures value different gifts and talents differently. Flourishing in Bronze Age Greece or the Iceland of the sagas was a different matter from flourishing in an Oxbridge common room. Still, it is also true that there are many ways *not* to flourish, and we can take it that in whatever cultural context he is set, the great-souled person is exceptionally able to avoid those.

What give us more trouble are this person's awareness of rank and hierarchy and his evident condescension to others. He is an elitist. If he is so simply because he is at the top of the social heap, then Russell's skepticism is in place, for this would be vanity rather than pride. We might sympathize more if instead we return to the association between pride and an awareness of having done something well, such as achieving excellence in some branch of art or science. Here persons of ability and understanding will, among other things, need to have a just estimate of their own abilities and understand that even if other people match them, some do not. How could they not? To become a distinguished pianist or scientist requires understanding what counts as distinction in those enterprises, constantly bearing it in mind, and constantly trying to implement it. It also requires judgment in what to undertake, refusing to waste time on trivial enterprises, or to become distressed at failure in enterprises that lie beyond one's current reach. The people who stand out will, as Aristotle says, care more about the opinion of equals than the plaudits of people who can't discriminate what is good from what is not. They know who is worth listening to. And to get where they are, they will need an acute eye or ear for not only the rare successes but also the many, many ways to fail in the enterprise.

This implies just self-confidence, but it does not imply vanity. Indeed, insofar as the adept's enterprises are worthwhile and admirable, it is more likely to imply due modesty. The adept measures himself against the grandeur of the undertaking, as implied in Newton's famous remark: "I do not know what I may appear to the world, but to myself I seem to have been only a boy playing on the sea-shore, and diverting myself in now and then finding a smoother pebble or a prettier shell than ordinary, whilst the great ocean of truth lay all undiscovered before me." The modesty Newton expresses is fitting, and can quite properly coexist with proper pride at having achieved things that deserve esteem and honor.[14] But proper pride in an achievement has nothing to do with vanity, which we have already located as either a ghastly superiority or more often greed for the envy of others.

I have talked a good deal about pride as awareness of a merit. But it is also important to recognize that pride can be a spur to achievement. We can try to do things for their own sake, but at least as often we try to do things because, we feel, we would "let ourselves down" if we failed the attempt. In the persona of Folly, Erasmus gives us a delightful, ironic description of this aspect of humanity. Folly is represented as having impregnated us with self-esteem or self-love:

> On the other hand if you have a low opinion of yourself, what can you do that is charming or graceful, what can you do that will not be indecorous and awkward? Take away Self-love, the very spice of life and immediately the orator with all his gestures will seem stale, the musician with all his harmonies will be hissed off the stage.... So needful is it that everyone should first be kind to himself, should flatter himself just a bit, should be a little pleased with himself, before he can be pleasing to others ... the chief point of happiness is to wish to be what you actually are.[15]

But where Folly talks of self-love as the impetus to great actions, it seems to me more appropriate to identify the motive as proper pride, or what might even be called self-respect. Milton makes this point in his rather quaint, biblical way:

> But there is yet a more ingenuous and noble degree of honest shame, or call it if you will an esteem, whereby men bear an inward reverence toward their own persons. And if the love of God as a fire sent from heaven to be ever kept alive upon the altar of our hearts, be the first principle of all godly and vertuous actions in men, this pious and just honouring of our selves is the second, and may be thought as the radical moisture and fountain head, whence every laudable and worthy enterprize issues forth.[16]

This, of course, is quite different from anything resembling either vanity or arrogance, for this kind of pride is not, at least on the surface, Rousseau's amour propre, arising from a comparison of oneself with others, but a kind of self-confidence arising from a comparison of our own strength with the tasks to be attempted, or a self-respectful, and perhaps pleasurable, reflection upon the magnitude of the tasks that have been successfully attempted. Yet the distance from amour propre is smaller than we might suppose, because one could have no measure of the degree of strength one has shown, or is intent upon showing, and no measure of the magnitude of actual or projected accomplishments, without an implicit comparison with what is normally within the human compass. Hume slyly makes this point against those who would praise God for the excellence of the cosmos. Since they have no other cosmos to compare with this one, they have no standard to offer to justify the praise: "Could a peasant, if the *Aeneid* were read to him, pronounce that poem to be absolutely faultless, or even assign to it its proper rank among the productions of human wit, he, who had never seen any other production?"[17]

Self-respect of the kind Milton is praising is a particular concern of ethicists writing in the Kantian tradition.[18] Kant associates it with the duty of self-improvement, the care of one's own soul, which also preoccupied many classical philosophers, and indeed those religious traditions that place a prime importance on one's own spiritual state. Far from being a selfish concern, as it might appear, this is thought to be the foundation without which it is impossible to respect others as morality requires. And we have already noticed that the converse, self-disgust or self-hatred, is unlikely to coexist with any great feeling for others and what they deserve. A cynical view of oneself is much more apt to consort with a similar view of others. Kant himself held that without duties to oneself, there could be no duties to others, although his reasoning is typically obscure.[19] One difficulty is that the duty of self-improvement is what he calls an "imperfect" duty, allowing a great variety of possible implementations (I don't have to try to learn every language or play every instrument), whereas many of the duties we owe to others are "perfect" duties resembling specific debts that require specific actions from us.

Aristotle talks more of virtue, which has a rather prissy ring to it. But he is best interpreted as simply transplanting these natural thoughts about excellence in any art or science into the more general business of life. And a particularly important element is the self-consciousness implied in his picture. The great-souled person is no innocent. He knows what he is doing and why, and so do other people.

As for his deep voice and measured gait, we might find ourselves agreeing with Lord Shaftesbury: "Gravity is of the very essence of imposture. It does not only make us mistake other things, but is apt perpetually almost to mistake itself."[20] This is why it is often irresistible to laugh at pomposity. But in the Aristotelian picture, the noble spirit is not an impostor and makes no mistake about himself. We need the Ciceronian notion of dignity, or measure or restraint, rather than pomposity. The great-souled man preserves decorum, but it might be quite decorous to romp with the grandchildren on the right occasion. So, allegedly, we ought to admire him rather than laugh at him.

A different and perhaps more urgent question is whether a culture itself values the activities in which greatness can be fought for, and understood. Consider, for instance, the difference between fine arts at the present time and (classical) music. Musicianship declares itself and admits few or no impostors. It requires talent and hard work, and a constant battle with the high peaks of the repertoire. It is founded on a craft skill, which is the ability to follow a set of instructions embedded in a score (or in the need to repeat or vary something just heard, if we consider skills other than sight-reading). Its finest exponents appear magical to the rest of us, and we willingly (I hope) allow them to have some right to behave as if great-souled. A Newtonian sense of the magnitude of their art will be part of that. By contrast fine art, alas, seems to be less secure. The art schools gave up craft a long time ago in favor of "expression," which is the aesthetic equivalent of supposing that strumming the piano puts you in a bracket with Beethoven, or that infantile babblings automatically scale the heights that were previously reserved for Shakespeare or Homer. It is the parent of innocent and boundless self-esteem. With all sense of standards or achievement gone, a cohort of cheerleaders does as well or better than success at anything more difficult to realize, such as expressing in a new way something deep or meaningful, dangerous or reassuring, about the human condition. In such a milieu, having no clothes will be a valid enough way of being an emperor. In such a milieu, vanity has to substitute for pride, and greatness of soul is best turned away at the door.

Is happiness the reward of virtue? Kant himself had little time for happiness as a goal in life. Given the critique of amour propre and the delusions attending the race up the greasy poles of wealth and power, we might sympathize with this neglect. But things are more complicated than this, and if you love yourself as you should, happiness is certainly on the horizon, although it takes a little work to bring it into focus. To do so we should contrast happiness with mindless euphoria. Aldous Huxley painted his people in *Brave New World* as able to enter such a state by taking the psychotropic drug "soma," which provided a "high" supposed to be like a cross between Christianity and alcohol, but without the downsides of either of them. But Huxley's world was an appalling dystopia in which all of the higher things in life—achievement, art, music, philosophy, religion, science—had been sacrificed to the social stability underpinning the endless sequence of mindless states of pleasure the inhabitants then enjoyed.

So weren't the people in *Brave New World* happy? Happiness is a complicated concept. If I meet my friends for an evening, we indeed want the evening to be a happy one, and will be pleased in proportion as it was so. But the crucial point is that we want our friends to be happy *at* certain things: speaking for myself, I hope that they are happy at me being with them, that they enjoy the conversation, that the food and wine are delightful, that together we enjoy the quick play and mutual delight of our minds being in harmony with one another. Suppose instead that I find them doped up with a vacant grin on their faces, happy-clappy, blindly euphoric, and stupidly grinning at everyone and everything. Suppose that even if I had brought them bad news, it would not have dinted their mindless bliss. Well, good for them—but this is not what we had hoped for when we set up the party or accepted the invitation. If those at the party are vacantly happy because of some version of soma, but not happy at being with me or with one another, then the evening is a write-off. It is important to our self-respect that we ourselves have been in some measure a part of their happiness, not just a cause of it (as we might be if, for instance, we had brought the drugs to the party), but in the far more important sense that our doings or our presence is the object of the pleasure.

The issues here lie deep within the philosophy of mind, where we have already seen that the child's awareness of itself is in part an awareness of others. If my conversation, or my doings, or my engagement with the company is an object of pleasure to them, it is because they are attentive to these things, responsive to them, and interacting with them, so that their pleasure at any moment is a function of this ebb and flow, and my reactions in turn are a function of theirs. A benignly euphoric presence in the corner may not actually detract from the evening but he or she is not part of this communal pleasure or communal happiness. A private euphoria, free-floating and indifferent to the state of the world around one, has something inane about it, which is the reason why we instinctively mistrust the promiscuous beam of the born-again or the evangelical nearly as much as we mistrust their solipsistic ranting. Soaked as they are in a complacent confidence of their own piety, their mindlessness may be nice for them, but not for us, for they have no intention of mirroring our minds but turn their backs on human engagement and human reciprocity. Parallel comments apply to the whole domain of the erotic, where an excitement that is due to drugs rather than to the partner is not nearly as satisfying to the partner as one that is not. A pleasure in someone else's pleasure in me is a very different thing from a mere awareness of someone else's impersonal pleasure. Nature itself warns us off: there is something false about a fixed grin, and we are very, very good at detecting one.

Company, then, is the sovereign remedy against desolation, boredom, self-obsession, and ultimate inanity. But as we have seen again and again, narcissism, vanity, and the arrogance that goes with them are the great enemies of togetherness. The narcissist set apart, the pouting figure on the catwalk, the plutocrat eaten with envy of others yet more plutocratic, are each of them prey to the worms that destroy "we" in favor of "I."

Yet "I" is not enough: the myth already told us that Echo is no fit companion for a human being.

7
Temptation

We have to start this chapter with a detour through the nature of religion. For if the Aristotelian great-souled man is poised, confident, dignified, and proud, the ideals of the Abrahamic religions offer us an astonishing contrast. The entire cosmos here seems to be structured by domination: on the one hand the Deity conceived as a lord or king, and on the other hand the subjects (us) whose nature is steeped in sin, and whose duty is abject obedience and submission. Just as the greatest sin in a monarchical society is treason against the monarch, so the sin that destroyed the cosmic harmony was rebellion and disobedience to God, and the root of this rebellion was pride. The only proper attitude we sinners ought to take toward God is servitude and resignation.

With the resurgence of respect for the classical world, this began to represent a highly unattractive ideal. As Rousseau said:

> Christianity preaches nothing but servitude and dependence. Its spirit is so favorable to tyranny that tyranny always profits from it. True Christians are made to be slaves. They know it and are scarcely moved thereby; this brief life is of too little worth in their view.[1]

In addition, any fleeting thought of superiority, or any closet complacency at being among the elect or the saints, must be sternly suppressed. There is also the curiosity, again noticed by Rousseau, that we are nevertheless supposed to love one another, even if the theology tells us that we are about as far from lovable as the preacher can imagine. No wonder the angel Lucifer protested against the whole setup, kicked over the traces, and took his satanic pleasure in getting the first woman, Eve, to join him.

Pursuing this vein we might add that the notion of sin is itself a moral concept corresponding to disgust, the appropriate reaction to uncleanliness and pollution. Since we all suffer from an inheritance of original sin, we also have a view of human life in which the pinnacle of virtue, that which corresponds to God's attitude toward us, is self-disgust, abasement, and humility, the drumbeat of unworthiness, the endless fear of our spiritual and bodily uncleanliness. We have the need for "redemption," an activity whose original meaning is the ransoming of a prisoner from captivity, and so we get the scrambled idea of a God paying a ransom to free us from sin and death, or in other words, from being captive to the human nature that he designed for us. It is with some relief that we turn to the Enlightenment to find adequate comment on all this:

> Celibacy, fasting, penance, mortification, self-denial, humility, silence, solitude, and the whole train of monkish virtues; for what reason are

> they everywhere rejected by men of sense, but because they serve to no manner of purpose; neither advance a man's fortune in the world, nor render him a more valuable member of society; neither qualify him for the entertainment of company, nor increase his power of self-enjoyment? We observe, on the contrary, that they cross all these desirable ends; stupefy the understanding and harden the heart, obscure the fancy and sour the temper. We justly, therefore, transfer them to the opposite column, and place them in the catalogue of vices; nor has any superstition force sufficient among men of the world, to pervert entirely these natural sentiments. A gloomy, hair-brained enthusiast, after his death, may have a place in the calendar; but will scarcely ever be admitted, when alive, into intimacy and society, except by those who are as delirious and dismal as himself.[2]

Hume speaks with all the poise of the man of the world (the last sentence would, I think, be a clear winner in a competition to find the perfect encapsulation of the spirit of the Enlightenment). By contrast, Nietzsche, just over a century later, cannot preach the message without becoming utterly apoplectic:

> I condemn Christianity. I raise against the Christian church the most terrible accusation that any accuser has ever uttered. It is to me the ultimate conceivable corruption. It has possessed the will to the final corruption that is even possible. The Christian church has left nothing untouched by its depravity: it has turned every value into a disvalue, every truth into a falsehood, every integrity into a vileness of the soul . . . .[3]

It is the resignation, the denial that life is there to be seized, the essentially cringing, humiliated tone of the Christian message that irritated him. Part of his irritation may have been directed against his teacher, Schopenhauer, whose quasi-Buddhist gospel of resignation perhaps outdid even that of Christianity.

But is Christianity really a religion of self-abasement, fit only to turn each of us into Uriah Heep? Flip the coin and any monotheistic religion looks like an extraordinary explosion of our own narcissism, pride, and vanity. It is not only that in the churches we find plausible exemplars of spiritual pride, but this is true in general: as it is said, God may have made man in his image, but man returned the compliment. We may live in our small corner of the universe, but God cares about us. Passionately. He has, perhaps, a rather mysterious way of showing it, but in this worldview, he notices *everything*. The all-seeing eye, untroubled by distance and distraction, is fixed on *me* and *you*. We are the center of its attention—and what higher pedestal can there be than that? Even the persona in the L'Oréal advertisement only gathers the attention of poor, deluded human beings, and aspirational ones at that. But *I* gather *his* attention. I am central to the concerns and love and (let us hope) the good opinion of the architect of the universe himself. That's most flattering, quite a pedestal in fact.[4]

Religious texts certainly recognize that this might be the efflorescence of pride rather than a road to due humility or awe. So we are reminded: "Are not two sparrows sold for a farthing? and one of them shall not fall on the ground without your Father."[5] God may care about me (hooray!), but then he cares about the sparrows equally as much (boo!). He has chosen people, it is true, but apparently he is an equal opportunity Father otherwise. Of course, how he juggles all these objects of concern has to remain a mystery to our poor, finite brains. If our biological father was as busy looking after eight-a-penny sparrows as he was looking after us when we scraped our knee, or got a bad mark on our homework, let alone when we lost our mother or when the earthquake or malaria or a thousand and one other ills struck us, we wouldn't feel too good. We wouldn't be too happy about that even if he added that he would make it all right for us later on, for instance, after we were dead.

This oscillation between an intently observant, caring, minutely engaged Father and a cosmically vast, infinite, timeless, unaffected, and therefore unconcerned Father is arguably essential to the religious condition. The two elements are played off with superb skill in Hume's last work, his great (and greatly entertaining) *Dialogues Concerning Natural Religion*. One of his theological spokesmen represents the former: the God of Abraham and Isaac, showing off his power, ordering things to happen, fussing around, making the odd miracle on behalf of his favorite people (ourselves), and, above all, bothered and concerned, often tweaking his own design for his own purposes. The other element represents the God of the philosophers: infinite, unchanging, unaffected, beyond comprehension, approachable only by going beyond expression—in one theological tradition, not even by poetry or music but only by silence.[6]

If on the one model God is a complete busybody and very dangerous, on the other model he has absconded completely. Although he was writing a century before Darwin, one of Hume's most telling problems with the former model is that while human passions are adaptations for our own natural and social relations in the particular empirical circumstances in which we find ourselves, God inhabits no such social, physical, or economic niche. Yet religionists attached to the God of Abraham and Isaac suppose that God nevertheless feels *just the same way* as we do. Like ourselves, he is jealous, envious, loving, vindictive, murderous, or forgiving, as the mood takes him. It's a bit surprising, since, for instance, he has nobody to envy, no competitors, no reason to blame people for the characters he gave them, and nothing to forgive except what he himself has created. The anger at his creation that Calvinists celebrated begins to look like the petulance of a small boy dissatisfied with whatever he has done with his Lego, except that unlike the small boy, God also made the Lego. Hume's spokesman for the God of the philosophers has no problem classifying this anthropomorphic, ruler-in-the-sky conception as almost blasphemous—little better than atheism.

On the other model God is beyond comprehension, infinite, unchanging, beyond time itself, unaffected ("actus purus" in the theological tradition, i.e., pure willing activity). He has no reality-receptive abilities at all: allegedly, he knows what to do without feedback or detection of the effects of his action. Here we meet other problems. The idea of an all-knowing God without any way of receiving information from the world is already more than a little perplexing. If he cannot witness things, touch them, hear them, then how does he know about them? And worse still, how does he know that he knows? Even if he is, luckily, right about what is going on, mightn't he quite reasonably be prey to the thought that all his ideas are those of a virtual reality of his own, with no independent existence? And then if God is, for instance, beyond time and not subject to change, why should we ourselves let our ideas about him influence our behavior? If he is indifferent, which, since he is unaffected by what we do, he is bound to be, then why should we go in for prohibitions, feasts or fasts, rituals, prayers, ceremonies, *words*, since none of them can make the least bit of difference? Any proponent of the anthropocentric God will now retort that this mysticism is itself little better than atheism. It makes little difference whether we say "we can understand nothing of the ultimate cause of the origin of the cosmos or of the laws that govern it" or whether we say "we can understand nothing of the ultimate cause *which is God*, of the origin of the cosmos or the laws that govern it." The words in italic are adding nothing of any use.

But now we must change gear. So far in this chapter we have been talking as if God is a further thing in the universe, a kind of superperson. This conception is characteristic of theology conceived of as "ontology," "ontotheology," or, in other words, a set of doctrines telling us about further dimensions to the world, further occupants of the world, and events that once happened to create or sustain the world, or that will literally happen, for instance, to ourselves in an afterlife. But many theologians take a quite different tack: they think of religious practice not in terms of new propositions to believe as literal truths about a new member of the world but as expressions of dimensions of ourselves. In the terms I quoted from Kant, religion is not about what nature makes of itself but about what human beings make of themselves. Its message is only one about how to live, or which attitudes to take to ourselves, other people, or the physical cosmos in which we find ourselves.

Since many people find it difficult to conceive of religion without ontotheology, or in other words, doctrines about the extra entity or entities inhabiting the universe, it is perhaps necessary to pause to explain the alternative. Most people know of religions, such as the purer forms of Buddhism, or Jainism in India, that exist without the doctrine of a personal guiding deity or deities. But they may find it puzzling to know what sets these apart as genuine religions, if this element of belief is lacking.

So let us think about this a little. The fire-breathing atheists about whom we have heard so much recently—the celebrated quartet of Richard Dawkins, Christopher Hitchens, Sam Harris, and Dan Dennett—think of religious commitments in terms of mistaken or at least hopelessly improbable and therefore irrational ontology. Believers think that something exists, but the overwhelmingly probable truth is that it does not. This is their take-home message. Yet this interpretation of the issue is itself mistaken, and indeed doubly so. It is mistaken, or perhaps it would be better to say unimaginative or off-key, to think of religious frames of mind primarily in terms of belief. And it is similarly misdirected to think that the belief component primarily concerns the existence of anything. Both these insights can be found in Hume's celebrated works on the philosophy of religion, but their lesson seems never to have been properly absorbed. Even Wittgenstein, I think, although he came close and certainly flirted with more adequate views, failed to take their measure properly.

To make both my claims plausible, we can contrast a religious frame of mind with a simple case of mistaken ontology. Russell once compared religious belief with the empirically absurd belief that there exists a teapot flying in its own extraterrestrial orbit around the sun, so this is a convenient example. Now the first obvious point is that nobody would think of belief in such a thing as itself religious. It has none of the hallmarks. It has nothing to do with the conduct of life, ethics, the formation of congregations, ritual, the sense of anything as sacred, consolation, hope, despair, or the many other emotional and social clothings of religion. It is simply a particularly daft secular belief.

But now suppose some of those clothings arrive. Imagine a tribe in which the teapot is important. The texts describing it are sacred. Out of its spout issue instructions for living. There are proper ways to show respect for it, cemented into services and rituals. There are sacred sites and taboos associated with it, and priests who interpret its sayings, or who alone are authorized to lift its hidden lid. It is anathema to mock it, or them. Many people assert that without the belief in the teapot, their lives would be meaningless. The teapot's rituals give them their consolations and their identity. They are part of the congregation that feels the same way. And so on and so on. The teapot has now become an object of veneration—a religious object.

Now my two claims can come further into focus. The first is that the religious clothing that arrived was not primarily a matter of belief. It was a matter of practical dispositions or stances toward things. It was partly like having a favorite poem in your head, or a preference for one kind of music or another. It was partly as well a commitment to some practices and some permissions and prohibitions: an immersion in a "way of life." The religious practice is a kind of social yoga that cements and fortifies our aesthetic and moral stances toward our lives and the world we live in.

My second claim is that the question of existence, the "ontology," has actually dropped out of the picture. It simply does not matter anymore whether there is such a teapot or not. A mythical teapot can perform the religious function of being a focus for emotions, attitudes, and social practices just as well as an actual teapot—better, in fact, since mythical teapots are not the objects of science. It will be no part of any religious practice to ask whether the teapot is pink or blue, how much it weighs, or how wide it is, any more than we ask the same kinds of questions about Zeus or Thor, Krishna or the World Serpent (Wittgenstein remarked that people who talk of God's all-seeing eye do not talk about his eyebrows). Teapot theologians would, rightly, be horrified at the idea of sending a spaceship to intercept the teapot: it is no part of the way of life associated with the picture that empirical confirmation or disconfirmation of that kind is remotely appropriate.

Hume said that religionists are in a "somewhat unaccountable" state of mind, somewhere between belief and disbelief. We can now see one thing that he may have meant. In my imagined tribe, the story about the teapot is serious—as serious as birth, death, marriage, togetherness, tribal identity, or any of the other aspects of living that the texts and rituals and ordained forms regulate and symbolize. It will not do to mock these things. On the other hand, it is empirically disengaged, or, if we like, empirically frivolous, for nothing empirical is relevant to its function as an intentional object, a focus for all the emotions and practices that the religious service of the teapot entails. A child can be afraid of the Jabberwock without really having any conception of it ("it seems to fill my head with ideas," said Alice, "but I do not know what they are"). Similarly, the religionist can venerate the teapot without any conception of it beyond a vague and changing kaleidoscope of imaginings. It is not these but his membership of the congregation that makes him a religionist.

We can now notice that the term "atheist," so carefully avoided by Hume himself, is no longer appropriate (whether we put the word "new" in front of it or not). It implies that there is a definite ontological belief that some people have and others do not, but this mislocates the issue. The term "agnostic" is no better, since it has the same implication of a definite ontological question, only one to which we do not know the answer.

Instead of waving theistic or atheistic banners, we should pick up Hume's *Natural History of Religion*, or its successors in the works of Kant, Feuerbach, Marx, or Durkheim. And if we want to wean people away from their myths, or the particular coloration their myths have taken at particular times and places, then we must do what Nietzsche did at the end of the nineteenth century, which was to recognize moral corruption when we find it, and then to rail, preach, inveigh, fulminate, or thunder against it.

So what we are really dealing with is not ontology and belief but anthropology and ways of life. There may be actual beliefs involved in the mix, such as historical beliefs about this and that, and these may be improbable and irrational, like creationists' idiotic beliefs about the geological timescale. Much more important, there may be much to dislike about contemporary ways of life that find Jesus of Nazareth as their focus, or Mohammed, Krishna, Buddha, or L. Ron Hubbard. Kant said that

> Even the Holy One of the Gospel must first be compared with our ideal of moral perfection before we can recognize him to be such; he also says of himself: Why do you call me (whom you see) good? No one is good (the archetype of the good) except the one God (whom you do not see).[7]

In other words, there is no escaping the burden of judgment: the fact that anything presented to our minds is capable of being judged good or bad. No text is so sacred that it escapes the jurisdiction of ethics, or what Iris Murdoch called the sovereignty of the good.

After surveying a great number of religions and religious practices worldwide, the French sociologist Émile Durkheim proposed the following account:

> A religion is a unified system of beliefs and practices relative to sacred things, that is to say things set apart and surrounded by prohibitions—beliefs and practices that unite its adherents in a single moral community called a church.[8]

According to Durkheim, shared religious rites and festivals serve both to cement the authority of the society and to energize its members through the consciousness of the force. For these effects to take place, it is only necessary that the participants expect them to take place: provided they are joyous at the festivals, awed at the presence of the sacred, obedient to the prohibitions and forms that surround the ritual, the practice will do its work. We might put it by saying that religious practice then inhabits the same shadowy yet intensely important niche as the placebo and nocebo effects. It is an area where thinking that something matters creates the psychological and social matrix in which it does matter. We are creatures who need ceremonies and rituals, not least to mark the passing of the years, births, comings of age, marriages, and death. If the rituals include music and poetry designed to take us out of ourselves, and if that is well done by invoking myths, songs, poetry, or even the infinities of space and time, it is not very wise for the philosophical atheist to protest too much.

Of course, the unifying effect need not be to make anything we would immediately call a congregation. It can just as easily make an army. Six centuries before Durkheim, the Islamic scholar Ibn Khaldun wrote:

> Vast and powerful empires are founded on a religion. This is because dominion can only be secured by victory, and victory goes to the side

> which shows most solidarity and unity of purpose. Now, men's hearts are united and coordinated, with the help of God, by participation in a common religion ... Religious fervor can efface the competitiveness and envy felt by the members of the group towards each other, and turn their faces towards the truth. When once their eyes have been fixed on the truth, nothing can stand in their way, for their outlook is the same and the object they desire is common to all and is one for which they are prepared to die ....[9]

Less devout than Ibn Khaldun, we might add that it is not necessarily orientation toward the truth that has this effect. Different stories will work the same effect for different tribes. We might also find it easier to draw the obvious implication that like any human practices, those of religions are not exempt from ethical questioning. Rituals and rites in groups change behavior, sometimes for the better, but sometimes for the worse. For the madness of crowds is a very close cousin to the fervor of congregations and the martial spirit of armies. Feelings are contagious, and get an orgiastic magnification through shared experiences, through empathetic identification with vast numbers of others, through mixtures of exhortation, music, poetry, movement, and drama. It may then be a matter of chance whether what follows is something sublime, such as peace, consolation, awe, elevation, and fellow-feeling, or something far from it, such as a renewed tribalism, race riot, lynch mob, crusade, or political rally. In the cold light of dawn, we might remember it with pleasure as exalted or with shame as nothing to be proud of.

On the other hand, I am not optimistic when political philosophers of a liberal persuasion may try to find authoritative principles proving that it is wrong for religionists to bring their faith-based moralities into the public sphere. I rather doubt that there are principles delivering this result, although it may be very desirable on other grounds. Insofar as they have separatist and tribal functions, religions should be kept out of the public square, but doing so is a political and cultural problem, not an intellectual one.

We might also want to return to Iris Murdoch and the way in which great art can take us out of ourselves. Inevitably, given the power and patronage of the Church, much of the great art of Western Europe before the Enlightenment was devoted to the glory of God. With Hume and Durkheim at hand, there remains no reason for atheists to starve themselves of it because of that. The glory of God symbolizes the emotions of human beings and the significant events in their lives: birth, death, marriage, friendship, betrayal, loss, and even forgiveness and redemption. Dr. Johnson pronounced that "that man is little to be envied whose patriotism would not gain force upon the plain of Marathon, or whose piety would not grow warmer among the ruins of Iona." We may not go so far, but we can go halfway. A piety toward the piety of others is a fairly minimal, undemanding kind of respect for the common humanity that we all share. Religions themselves would be better if they managed to promote it worldwide.

With this detour through the philosophy of religion completed, we can return in a more sympathetic mood to the Christian suspicion of pride. So just as we started with the myth of Narcissus, now we finish with an even more cosmic, epic, and endlessly reinterpretable myth, that of the Fall, and I shall enlist Milton to help us explore it. The superficial trappings of his great story of temptation and fall are not ones to which secularists give much houseroom, but once we have got beyond ontotheology, they are not the point of the allegory either. Like other works of its kind, such as sixteenth-century poet Edmund Spenser's *Faerie Queene* or John Bunyan's *Pilgrim's Progress*, Milton uses the supernatural forces and persons in the allegory to bring us to some knowledge about ourselves. If we take one of these earlier works as an introductory example, we find Spenser having his hero come to the House of Pride:

> A stately Pallace built of squared bricke,
> Which cunningly was without morter laid,
> Whose wals were high, but nothing strong, nor thick,
> And golden foile all over them displaid,
> That purest skye with brightnesse they dismaid:
> High lifted up were many loftie towres,
> And goodly galleries farre over laid,
> Full of faire windowes and delightful bowres;
> And on the top a Diall told the timely howres.
> It was a goodly heape for to behould,
> And spake the praises of the workmans wit;
> But full great pittie, that so faire a mould
> Did on so weake foundation ever sit:
> For on a sandie hill, that still did flit
> And fall away, it mounted was full hie,
> That every breath of heaven shaked it:
> And all the hinder parts, that few could spie,
> Were ruinous and old, but painted cunningly.[10]

The symbolism is obvious enough: lofty pride is associated with deceptive, superficial glitter, with lack of solidity and foundation, and with ruinous hidden aspects, the bits that are not in the shop-window, as it were, but that are associated with despair and ruin.

Similarly, Milton's story of the Fall is an allegory. It is timeless, and what it represents are temptations and pitfalls that beset human beings everywhere, all the time. It is for the "guilty reader" to recognize himself in Adam and Eve, and there is ample evidence in a close reading of the poem that this is exactly what Milton has offered us.[11] Readers are themselves to be entangled, sucked in by Satan's temptations, in order to recognize their own fallen human nature. So if we can learn from any drama of weakness, temptation, vice, or redemption, we can learn from this one, whether we think of ourselves as religious or not. Taking the myth as an allegory then, we need to find a message by abstracting away from the actual dramatis personae—Adam, Eve, Satan, God, and, of course, the whole troupe of supporting angels and devils. We need to approach the story as one symbolizing something about ourselves, and it ought to be something more powerful and interesting than the fact that wrongdoing can be frightfully tempting, or that we can deceive ourselves that it is all right after all.

As in the myth of Narcissus, we certainly find much to recognize. For example, Eve goes through both the kinds of vanity we earlier distinguished. Her creation in the Garden of Eden is first followed by narcissistic admiration of herself:

> As I bent down to look, just opposite,
> A Shape within the watry gleam appeerd
> Bending to look on me, I started back,
> It started back, but pleas'd I soon returnd,
> Pleas'd it returnd as soon with answering looks

> Of sympathie and love, there I had fixt
> Mine eyes till now, and pin'd with vain desire,
> Had not a voice thus warnd me, What thou seest,
> What there thou seest fair Creature is thy self . . . [12]

Pure Narcissus. But Eve is better than this, and soon puts narcissism behind her when she comes face-to-face with Adam and naturally enough is overcome by his beauty (writing in a prefeminist age, Milton assures us, less convincingly, that his is a superior beauty, but this is at least in part beauty of mind, since he is also said to be wiser than Eve). However, in the dream that foreshadows her fall, Satan, "squat like a toad," tempts her with the second kind of vanity, amour propre, or greed for the envy of others. Satan is discovered trying to raise

> At least distemper'd, discontented thoughts,
> Vain hopes, vain aimes, inordinate desires
> Blown up with high conceits ingendring pride.[13]

These thoughts are whispered into Eve's ear as she sleeps. On awakening, she repudiates them, but they do not go away. We can imagine them silently working away, and eventually they transform themselves into full-blooded ambition.

Eve's dream is a theologically odd episode, for before the Fall she is supposed to be in paradise. And yet even here Eve has troubled dreams of ambition and vanity; even here the idea of temptation is possible. Allied to this we can notice that, considered as ontotheology, Milton's drama of the arrival of evil in the world does not really work, because the evil that befalls Adam and Eve and their descendants (us) is predated and explained only by the evil rebellion of Satan and his crew of associates, and there is no sufficient story about how pure goodness could be the fountainhead and origin of that. It is just a given that God's train of angels, his perfect creation, should contain rotten elements. Certainly, there are attempts to pass this off as the result of a "freedom" in God's creatures, but this can hardly be the last word, since God also foresees the way in which his creatures would use that freedom, and there is no evident reason why he should not have created some free creatures rather nicer than we are. In any event, as Hume and many others have pointed out, only a fraction of the ills that beset mankind are due to whatever freedom we may be said to have and the bad choices we then make. Disease, mortality, accidents, earthquakes, and tidal waves beset us whatever we choose. If we read Milton's poem as a philosophical attempt to explain how a perfect deity created an imperfect world, it inevitably fails.

Anyhow, as far as poor Eve is concerned, Satan is hovering at her ear from the beginning. She is never going to be entirely free of the fancies or imaginings that will eventually have her succumbing to temptation. And in the successful drama of corruption that eventually follows, Satan returns straight to Eve's weakest point: her vanity. He points out to Eve that the apple is just the thing to elevate her into an angelic or godlike status—"for look," he lies, "it has turned me, a mere snake, into half way to being a human being, having the power of speech." Then the voice in her head, the voice to which she listens, tells her:

> Fairest resemblance of thy Maker faire,
> Thee all things living gaze on, all things thine
> By gift, and thy Celestial Beautie adore
> With ravishment beheld, there best beheld

> Where universally admir'd; but here
> In this enclosure wild, these Beasts among,
> Beholders rude, and shallow to discerne
> Half what in thee is fair, one man except,
> Who sees thee? (and what is one?) who shouldst be seen
> A Goddess among Gods, ador'd and serv'd
> By Angels numberless, thy daily Train.[14]

The serpent at this point, we are told, appears irresistibly, toweringly magnificent. The glittering temptation appeals exactly to Eve's lurking conceit that she is really rather special, and therefore it is simply not good enough to be admired by just a few beasts and one man. In other words, precisely like L'Oréal's temptation, Satan's works by showing Eve a pedestal, telling her that she is worth far more than she is stuck with at present, and raising "inordinate desires." Of course, Satan is lying since Eve is not the fairest resemblance of her Maker (as we have been told, Adam is), and neither should she aspire to be more than human, a Goddess among Gods, or an object of adoration to angels. But the lie works.

According to the classic analysis of Stanley Fish, the whole poem is what theologians term a "good temptation," which, according to Milton, is "that whereby God tempts even the righteous for the purpose of proving them, not as though he were ignorant of the disposition of their hearts, but for the purpose of exercising or manifesting their faith or patience . . . or of lessening their self-confidence, and reproving their weakness, that . . . they themselves may become wiser by experience."[15] The reader, in other words, is lured into himself questioning the ways of God, himself finding unjustifiable the arbitrary command not to touch the particular tree, and himself finding plausible Satan's beguiling arguments telling Eve that she can surely ignore the command, and indeed that it is undignified and unworthy to feel bound by it. And when we recognize that we are so tempted, we are intended to pause, take stock, recognize our kinship with Eve, and presumably resolve to do better. In other words, according to Fish, the whole poem is subtly self-undermining. It is not a failure of Milton that he cannot solve the problem of Evil, or is unable to "justify the ways of God to man," since his real purpose is otherwise. It is to have the reader question his own desire for such a justification, or his own pride and his own weak faith in a benign providence, when confronted with the world's evils.

This would be entirely satisfactory if all the elements of the story fit easily into an allegorical reading, but it is not entirely plain sailing. The first elements of the story that we might find it difficult to interpret are then those that concern *commands*, *obedience*, and *hierarchy*. Why are these the elements that set the scene? As we saw earlier, there is no identity or close connection between pride and disobedience: Is this just a peculiar obsession of the monotheistic religions?

The answer is implicit in the function of religious practice that we have seen highlighted by Durkheim, whereby it is adapted to emphasizing the rights of the society against those of the individual. Religious practices then include the arbitrary signification of certain things or places as consecrated or sacred, and reserved to some particular, selected members of the group, such as elders or priests, males or females. Inducted into such practices the individual learns of the power of the social order, it being not uncommon for it to be a serious crime, or even a capital offense, to trespass against the taboos surrounding whatever is reserved as sacred. The appropriate response to this power is exactly one of unquestioning obedience and submission. The voice of the collective is magnified by ritual obedience and insistence. It becomes unthinkable for the adept to transgress against the norms. So it is not surprising that when the story is mythologized, the central element is the same imperative voice, although the cost, to the ontotheologian, is that the persona of God appears arbitrary and tyrannical.

That is just the ontotheologian's problem, however. Take the myth as an allegory and it all falls much more neatly into place. The very arbitrariness of a consecration or a ritual also becomes a badge of belonging. Insiders know these things; outsiders do not. In *Monty Python and the Holy Grail*, the questing knights affirm their identity by proclaiming "we are the knights who say 'ni'"—an absurd, but in the light of Durkheim's insights, utterly recognizable, instance of a peculiarity that sets them apart, and the need for some such peculiarity may be common to all human groupings.

Quite apart from Durkheim's insight into the social function of such practices, we can also identify the moral in terms of the authority not of the tribe but of duty, the right, or the good. Conscience is the aspect of our emotional and practical nature that makes us receptive to the thought that something has to be done, or must not be done, or is in some way demanded of us. And to work as it should, this recognition has to come as authoritative, or possessing the right to precedence over our other desires or temptations. The voice of conscience is not to be ignored: we may want to do one thing or another, but if it tells us that we must not, then obedience is the required response. Above all, conscience commands. If conscience is then understood as the inner candle, the light of the Lord illuminating ourselves from within, it is no wonder that the principal response to the God who has this as his echo inside us is to be obedience and submission. This is misinterpreted if conscience is thought of as sufficiently mysterious, sufficiently apart from the rest of our psychology, to suggest some kind of supernatural or divine origin and sanction by itself. It is we, acting together, with the authority of the collective, who put ourselves under what the philosopher Allan Gibbard calls a system of "normative governance" and who feel (or ought to feel) the pressure of any particular rule of behavior and the discomfort of trespassing against it.[16]

This may also help to understand the next problematic aspect of the myth. Why is it knowledge—or, in particular, the knowledge of good and evil—that is forbidden to Adam and Eve? If on reflection we thought there is something bad about knowledge as such, this would make immediate sense. If this were so, then being good would require maintaining innocent ignorance, and this is naturally enough allegorized in terms of a command forbidding us from eating the fruit of that particular tree. But if we cannot share this view, it is not just that we will be tempted to admire Satan's argument that God's command is an arbitrary exercise of tyranny, but we will be right to think it. If the point of this feature of the allegory is that knowledge is a Bad Thing, then we are within our rights to reject it.

The Gnostic tradition does indeed reject it. In this heretical view, the God of Genesis is the Jehovah of the Old Testament, and by no means good. He made the rotten world and issued the arbitrary commands so the real heroes are those with the courage to disobey, just as Prometheus is the hero who disobeys Jupiter or Zeus's command by bringing fire to mankind. It is easy to draw the same conclusion from Calvinist theology, in which God has arbitrarily predestined some people to hell and others to salvation, regardless of how they behave in the here and now. Calvinists may try to repeat to themselves that this was an exercise of Divine justice, but the rival view, that it must have been the doing of either an impotent or an uncaring deity, is a good deal more plausible. Gnostic views grumble on within more orthodox Christian theology, anticipating the later Romantic idea that Satan is the hero of the myth, and Jehovah or the controlling deity the insufferable tyrant (the parallel is central to Shelley's poem *Prometheus Unbound*). In the versions of the Gnostic tradition known as Ophism, the serpent can actually be identified with Jesus Christ, for since knowledge is good, whatever leads us to it is also good.[17]

There is certainly an element in our traditions that debates to what extent the human thirst for knowledge and understanding is admirable, and the monotheistic religions of the West are often ambivalent about it. In the Old Testament, the book Ecclesiastes implies that the desire for knowledge is itself just a particular kind of vanity, and although the story that the caliph Omar ordered the destruction of the great library at Alexandria on the grounds that there was no need for anyone to read any other text than the Qur'an is apocryphal, its currency suggests that such an event would not be beyond the bounds of possibility. The myth of Faustus, whose knowledge is acquired through a pact with the devil, is itself an allegory on the vanity of wanting to know too much, and this is not just a preoccupation of monotheistic religion, since, as we have already noted, in classical antiquity the gods punished Prometheus for bringing the knowledge of fire to mankind, while Icarus, the son of the master craftsman Daedalus, was destroyed by flying too close to the sun.

Yet even if it is common, the idea that knowledge is generally bad, dangerous, or a symptom of vanity is surely unsustainable. The exigencies of human life mean that it is typically better to know than not to know. Knowing whether there is a predator in one place or foodstuff in another made life possible, while every human group has to know a good amount about how to hunt, plant, cultivate, cook, construct, and travel, as well as to know what to select and promulgate, or avoid and condemn.

Following Nietzsche, the philosopher Bernard Williams reflected on the more general human desire to know not just things we can exploit in the here and now, the immediate environment within which we have to act if we are to survive, but also to know things about distant places and events. Refusing to put up with myths and falsehoods, for instance about history, might have no immediate payoff, and societies can survive quite comfortably wrapped in a cocoon of fantasy about their origins and evolution, and the events that brought them where they are. Scotsmen may after all be disappointed to learn that the "clan tartan" was a nineteenth-century invention, and it is more comfortable for most nations to turn a blind eye to many of their own past doings. In both Britain and the United States, as well as Belgium, France, and Germany, a nicely whitewashed version of their colonial history is good deal more comfortable than anything that saturates the colors. We do not enjoy learning how the White Man's Burden tended to be carried by the colonized people. Nietzsche noticed that it is therefore a remarkable thing that we should care to get these things right, or as right as we can. It is the mark of an "ascetic ideal," and the scientist or historian's will to truth is as much an ascetic practice or disposition as the priest's vow of chastity or the vegetarian's renunciation of meat. But it is an admirable ideal for all that. The lazy acceptance of falsity is a vice, not a virtue.

So once more, why is the forbidden fruit hanging on the tree of knowledge? A false step is surely to think of it simply in terms of the arrival of sexual knowledge, a particular obsession of Western theologians. These have, for instance, troubled themselves with whether there were sexual relations in paradise before the Fall. Some, like Saint Thomas Aquinas, hazarded that Adam and Eve did not have sufficient time to get into bed before they took the apple, although others, such as Saint Augustine, grasped the nettle, allowed that sexual activity must have occurred, but hazarded bizarre views about what it might have been like.[18] Milton at least is quite clear about it and about its enormous pleasurability. His lines describing it are among the most lyrical and erotic in English literature (4.736–75). So it is not mere acquaintance with sexuality that is the problem. Indeed, the angel Raphael explains to Adam that in spite of being disembodied, angels too have their own modes of mingling together, although surprisingly enough he blushes as he says it (8.618–29). Blushing is a sign of embarrassment, a younger sibling of shame, so it is actually quite unclear what Raphael's problem can be. Shame is a reaction to things one fears to be sins, faults, or flaws. It had no place in Eden before the Fall, so presumably it ought not to have a place in heaven either.

In the myth the immediate effect of eating the apple is that discord and shame come into paradise. Once Adam and Eve have lost their pristine innocence, they rapidly begin to quarrel, and their sexual relations, hitherto conducted in the rather childlike state of pleasure that 1960s flower children sought to recover—making sex pretty much comparable to eating ice cream—instead become fraught with a great deal of difficulty and shame. It seems then that gaining knowledge of good and evil is rather akin to growing up, emerging from a Peter Pan state of enjoyment of whatever pleasures are at hand into an adult state of having to weigh consequences, resist temptations, and bow to the norms of conduct that in fact hedge any kind of sexual life, or any kind of social life. But that in turn seems incompatible with the tradition's undoubted insistence that there is something both deliberate about it and bad about it. It cannot be Adam and Eve's fault that they grow up. *That* cannot be the sin into which they were tempted and for which they need redemption.

Perhaps instead we should ask whether the disturbing lack of specificity is integral to the myth. This might be in two ways. First, returning to Durkheim, we may remember the element of arbitrariness in the rites and prohibitions associated with consecration of things and places. A society would not be glued together by, for instance, a shared awareness that some fungi, tempests at sea, or precipitous journeys at night are dangerous. Such awareness would obviously be the common property of insiders and outsiders alike, and just because of that, it would lack the essentially arbitrary and conventional import that would be hidden from those who are not initiated, and bind together those who are. We can be bound into a fellowship by knowing that we are the knights who say "ni," whereas we cannot be bound by knowing that we are the knights who try not to fall over cliffs. Understood cautions would not bind insiders in a way that fortifies them against outsiders; arbitrary, culturally manicured rites and habits do so.

Second, just because the Fall is so indeterminate, it is fit to stand for any and every fall. There is a sense that every time we succumb to a specific evil temptation, we gain an iota of knowledge of good and evil, whether it is through greed, envy, lust, pride, hate, cruelty, or anything else. We become acquainted with possibilities within ourselves that we might prefer not to have been forced to acknowledge. Sin carries increased self-knowledge, albeit guilty, ashamed, or even despairing self-knowledge, in its very nature. To put it another way, once the ontological trappings of the myth are abandoned, we have simply an abstract template, a *shape* of any and every temptation: the unfolding or manifestation of a disposition to fall.

Confirmation of this interpretation of the myth is found in many of the marvelous details with which Milton describes the events surrounding Eve's trespass. After laying the groundwork, as it were, by visiting her sleep and dreams, unconsciously preparing Eve for the full-scale assault, we have the appeal to her vanity, quoted above. We also have Satan's dismissal of the importance of the prohibition, corresponding to the easy self-justifications we give ourselves for doing what we really know we should not do:

> . . . will God incense his ire
> For such a petty trespass, and not praise
> Rather your dauntless virtue?[19]

We have the increasing attraction of the forbidden fruit, which begins to work on Eve's senses:

> Meanwhile the hour of noon drew on, and wak'd
> An eager appetite, raised by the smell
> So savorie of that Fruit, which with desire,
> Inclinable now grown to touch or taste
> Solicited her longing eye.[20]

Her own rationalization, succumbing to Satan's argument, follows, and then:

> So saying, her rash hand in an evil hour
> Forth reaching to the Fruit, she plucked, she eat.[21]

There is a marvelous psychological insight here, later rediscovered by Jean-Paul Sartre. Far from being entirely in charge, at the very moment of decision, we can seem almost to have abdicated: we are tempted, the temptation expands, we dither—and then our hand moves and the thing is done. Sartre said that "when I deliberate the die is already cast—the decision has already been taken, by the time the will intervenes." It is as if an automatic pilot takes over. Or, as preachers like to remind us, you fall in the direction you're leaning. But far from absolving us from responsibility, that is just what exercising responsibility is like. It was Eve who ate the apple, not some onboard control system distinct from herself. We might think that by the time the groundwork has been laid, Eve "could not help herself," but Milton, at least, is clear that this affords no kind of excuse. Her responsibility lay in the whole train of events, from the dream onward. We do not find it in a snapshot of the moment that her rash hand reaches out. She is to blame for being the kind of person who heard those serpent voices in her head, and succumbed to their seduction.[22]

Succumbing to temptation is absolutely delicious in the short run, and Milton gives us this as well. "Back to the thicket slunk the guilty serpent"—as well he should, since his work is over, while Eve

> Intent now wholly on her taste, naught else
> Regarded, such delight till then, as seemed,
> In Fruit she never tasted, whether true
> Or fancied so, through expectation high
> Of knowledge.[23]

The world seems just fine immediately after we have quaffed the extra glass of wine that we should not have had, whizzed safely through the red light, or started an illicit liaison with the dishy but unfortunately married person at the photocopier. This may be only a "seeming," says Milton. In other words, we may actually be deceiving ourselves about the extent of the pleasure. But for the moment, it feels terrific: we not only have the apple, but we have been brave enough to get it. We have trodden down cowardly scruples, become a little heroic, made a little stand against the stifling voices of conformity, and what a pleasure there is in that! The cost comes later. The same rhythm is repeated when Adam, knowing (unlike Eve) that he is doing wrong, follows suit and eats the apple:

> As with new Wine intoxicated both
> They swim in mirth, and fansie that they feel
> Divinity within them breeding wings
> Wherewith to scorn the earth . . .[24]

Succumbing to temptation is simply delicious, and the more so precisely because of its transgressive feel. Hume makes the same point:

> Hence we naturally desire what is forbid, and take a pleasure in performing actions, merely because they are unlawful. The notion of duty, when opposite to the passions, is seldom able to overcome them; and when it fails of that effect is apt rather to increase them, by producing an opposition in our motives and principles.[25]

The "opposition" Hume speaks of is a kind of enlivening, an increased vitality or animation, which Spinoza had associated with an increase of well-being or happiness. Hume gives another example of the same effect in the ways in which a skilled orator will play hide-and-seek with his audience:

> 'Tis certain nothing more powerfully animates any affection than to conceal some part of its object by throwing it into a kind of shade, which at the same time that it shows us enough to prepossess us in favour of the object leaves still some work for the imagination. Besides that obscurity is always attended with a kind of uncertainty; the effort which the fancy makes to complete the idea, rouses the spirits, and gives an additional force to the passion.[26]

To put it more bluntly, a striptease is more arousing than a nudist beach.

I believe that collecting all this together does much to justify the choice of disobedience as the paradigm of succumbing to temptation. It is not that there is a personal tyrant set over us. Rather, it is we ourselves who judge that we ourselves, or other people, are guilty of falling, when we do. To suppose this, it has to be we ourselves who are exercising a system of norms that do not permit the trespass. Adhering to a system of norms is, in turn, to suppose some things to be permissible and others to be forbidden. Lying, breaking promises, manipulating others, taking advantage of the weak, humiliating and otherwise causing pain are just a few of the things most of us regard as forbidden. So anyone guilty of them is in effect disobeying an imperative or command not to do such things. Hence, bad behavior is naturally thought of as a species of disobedience, and it opens up to the punishment of a bad conscience, or the punishment of social sanction.

Hence as well, if pride is located as a kind of rebellion against being subject to a command, then it takes its place as the overarching pattern or template of wrongdoing or sin. It is not just another sin alongside, say, greed or envy. It is better to see it as having the role of the activator or catalyst, the trait that allows the greed to go ahead or that makes room for the envy. There is therefore an insight in saying, as the tradition does, that when it so acts, pride is the "radix omnium malorum," the root of all evil. Other things, such as stupidity, greed, and delusion, certainly nourish evil all by themselves. But pride is the catalyst that precipitates the Fall, and as such it may well deserve a preeminent place.

8

Integrity, Sincerity, Authenticity

These are not, strictly speaking, emotions, let alone emotions particularly concerned with self-assessments or self-love. But they are closely related to feelings about ourselves. They are connected with the kind of pride that we have seen valued by Aristotle, Milton, and Kant, the kind that goes along with sufficient self-respect to motivate fine or noble behavior, or at least to ward off base and ignoble behavior. They each have a positive ring. They stop us from letting ourselves down.

Integrity especially implies a kind of unity or wholeness, a lack of fault lines or divisions. "Here I stand," said Martin Luther, ringing true as a bell, "I can do no other." We might think of the familiar Hollywood hero, unflinching, principled, and literally unable to follow the mean or cowardly path. We thrill to the moment when the hero, in spite of temptations and difficulties, reveals his true colors, blazes forth in a kind of transfiguration, rises to do what has to be done, and with steady hand and clear eye walks out erect to confront (and overcome) the overwhelming odds stacked against him. We admire him, of course, and wish we would be like him, and perhaps fear that we would not measure up. Our minds would be divided. Part of us would want to find an excuse and duck out.

It is not that the man or woman of integrity is immune to misfortune in the way that the Stoics hoped. Indeed, they are particularly vulnerable to one very serious kind of misfortune. A lapse in integrity fractures the whole edifice of their personality. It would strike at the heart of their self-identity or self-esteem. If Luther can do no other, it is because his whole self stands in the way; were he to fall or to fail, the result would be a personal catastrophe. This might be so even if the fall or failure is no fault of his or her own. In Shakespeare's *Rape of Lucrece*, the heroine literally cannot continue to live once her honor has been violated, although she did nothing to abet the violation and everything within her power to prevent it. Integrity implies the direct opposite of the "Hey, let's move on" insolence or carelessness of the wrongdoing politician or narcissist whom we met earlier. It implies that with a fracture, there can be no recovery, no moving on.

The danger with this ideal, as with that of Stoicism, with which we started, is that it easily consorts with something rather different, and far from ideal. Isn't the hero a little too, well, cardboard? Is the undivided mind just a little too unimaginative? Aldous Huxley thought so, writing that "single-mindedness is all very well in cows or baboons; in an animal claiming to belong to the same species as Shakespeare it is simply disgraceful." Inflexibility is not one of the more obvious or attractive virtues. Perhaps it is only inflexibility in pursuit of the Good that is always a virtue. But then, is the undivided mind particularly skilled at exercising the delicate balancing that is often necessary to discover where the Good lies? The film or fiction of the kind I have indicated makes this easy: the bad guys and the bad courses are dressed in black and the good ones in white, and after the denouement, everyone good lives happily ever after. But real life is not so easy.

The most celebrated discussion of integrity in recent philosophy comes from Bernard Williams, who was particularly concerned to contrast the virtue with the kind of means-end, consequentialist reasoning that utilitarianism recommends. Williams offered two scenarios.[1] In one, an explorer, Jim, in a rather unpleasant part of the world, stumbles upon a village where an army officer is about to shoot twenty of the (innocent) inhabitants. However, in honor of his guest, the officer offers to let the rest go if Jim will shoot one, and we can stipulate that the relevant consequences are measured by the body count. Williams is not concerned to argue that utilitarianism gives the wrong answer to this dilemma. His complaint is rather that it asks Jim to answer too easily: for the utilitarian or consequentialist, it should be obvious what to do, and Jim need not hesitate. But, of course, it is plausible that Jim would hesitate a good deal: he might, and perhaps should, feel that his own sense of himself, his identity, would be violated by shooting an innocent person, and we can easily imagine that if he does so, then the whole thing would become an indelible trauma, and his conscience or memory would give him little rest. Williams's other scenario has a similar structure. George is a chemist, deeply opposed to chemical warfare but faced with the option of taking a job in a chemical warfare institute. He and his family need the money, and, furthermore, he knows that if he does not take the job, a colleague who is zealous for promoting chemical warfare will do so, while if he takes it, he can very likely delay, impede, or redirect any advances in the technology. Again, consequences point one way, but George's scruples and principles will and should prevent him from finding this a simple decision. In Williams's terms it can seem like an assault on one of the "ground plans" of his life: not to kill innocent people in Jim's case, and it is not to promote the means of doing so in George's.

These cases have provoked a great deal of discussion. Their value in undermining utilitarianism is easy to challenge: if people live by a set of values other than those recommended by any moral theory, T, then they may feel discomfited or destabilized by being asked to drop those values and abide by T instead. But that hardly seems like a reason for supposing that T is the wrong theory. I would say, for instance, that the duty to assist someone needing emergency help outweighs any religious prohibition on stirring yourself on a particular day. But I can imagine people finding it very difficult, an assault on their identity or their integrity, to break the prohibition, particularly if it has been inculcated in them from childhood. We might at some level admire them for finding it difficult—it is, after all, a loyalty to their beloved parents or culture—but without for a moment supposing that they are right to withhold the assistance.

Again, it is only a very simple form of utilitarianism that finds itself in Williams's target area. More sophisticated forms (including that of John Stuart Mill in his classic essay) stress the overwhelming utility of dispositions and habits of motivation. And among those, a reluctance to get involved in a killing, or a reluctance to promote horrible armaments, would obviously rank very high. We think the world will go better if people shrink from performing what would normally be intolerable actions, even if this makes it difficult for them in the extraordinary circumstances specified in the thought experiment.

This brings us to a final question we can ask of Williams's cases. Quite what kind of integrity is he asking us to admire? Is the agent's integrity (wholeness, undividedness) supposed to render the occasion simple? In other words, should we admire for his integrity the Jim who simply turns his back on the possibility of saving the nineteen villagers? And what about the religious adept who single-mindedly ignores tragedies he could prevent or at which he could assist, if they occur on one of the holy days when he must not stir himself? Integrity here looks as if it turns into blindness, or self-indulgence. It is not always virtuous to be single-minded when the world throws its complex situations at us. Our "personal projects" or even our "ground plans" do not deserve an authority that licenses deafness to everything else that may clamor for our help.

It has also been pointed out that the problems of what to do afflict utilitarians as much as anyone else, and perhaps more chronically than those following a simple ethic of prohibitions and permissions.[2] A utilitarian who conceives us as under an obligation to do what we can for the good of others soon faces the difficult question of how stringent this duty of charity should be allowed to become. Most of us want space for our own doings, and if we are richer than many others in the world, our own doings will include spending money on ourselves and our nearest and dearest. But that money could surely have done more good for human happiness had it been channeled toward alleviating some of the appalling afflictions that the poor of the world labor under. A utilitarian of real integrity, one might think, should be willing to donate far more than most of us do to relieve those afflictions. He would want to become a "servant of the world," sacrificing his own partial concerns for the good of the greatest number. If one of Williams's aims in presenting his thought experiments was to ring-fence a legitimate area of private interests, enabling the virtuous person to resist the escalation of duty that true charity might demand, then a more strenuous moralist might say that however natural and tempting it is to follow him, the thorny path of virtue points in a different direction. We might have our big houses, fancy restaurants, fast cars, and medical featherbedding, but it is by no means clear that we should have them with a spotless conscience as well.

The upshot, then, is that integrity is by no means the unalloyed good that it might seem to be. It has too many connotations of simple-minded one-word solutions to what ought to be felt as intractable and difficult dilemmas. There is an interesting reversal here: Williams's original complaint was that Jim and George ought to find their dilemmas harder than they would appear to a utilitarian; but widening our gaze we find that it is more likely to be the person of any unconflicted, simple creed who becomes ill-adapted to reflect as he should, or to respond as he should, to the manifold complexities of any kind of mature life. It is enviable to be as sound as a bell, but not if the bell tolls the death knell of ambivalence and conflict in our more educated and imaginative responses.

Further depth can be added to these reflections if we turn (as Williams himself insisted that we should) to the history of concepts such as sincerity, integrity, and authenticity. The starting point for this history is the famous opposition that Hegel introduced, between classical drama and modern drama from the Renaissance. The former concerns the conflict of objective, authoritative, moral principles, but this shifts in the modern period to a concentration on personality, the locus not of great principles but of a kind of subjective chaos of personal forces. We do not have to pronounce on the overall value of this scheme, but it is revealing to think of integrity in the light of it. Thus, the classical scholar Bernard Knox writes of the heroes of the dramas of Sophocles:

> In a Sophoclean drama we are never conscious, as we always are with Aeschylus, of the complex nature of the hero's action, its place in the sequence of events over generations past and future, its relation to the divine plan of which that sequence is the result. The Sophoclean hero acts in a terrifying vacuum, a present which has no future to comfort and no past to guide, an isolation in time and space which imposes on the hero the full responsibility for his own action and its consequences. It is precisely this fact which makes possible the greatness of the Sophoclean heroes; the source of their action lies in them alone, nowhere else; the greatness of the action is theirs alone. Sophocles presents us for the first time with what we recognize as a "tragic hero": one who, unsupported by the gods and in the face of human opposition, makes a decision which springs from the deepest layer of his individual nature, his *physis*, and then blindly, ferociously, heroically maintains that decision even to the point of self destruction.[3]

Knox here suggests that it is out of a kind of metaphysical vacuum, unguided by the gods or by the world, that the Sophoclean hero forges an obsessive principle of action. This needs a little qualification. In *Antigone*, for instance, the heroine conceives of herself as under a necessity to bury her dead brother, Polyneices, who was killed while mounting a treasonable coup against their home city, Thebes, and its ruler, Creon. This necessity is presented as holy, sanctioned by the gods of the underworld. It is indeed Antigone herself who "puts on the yoke of necessity," but the yoke is supposed to exist objectively, in the nature of things, as it were.[4] It is not supposed simply to spring from a decision or quirk of Antigone herself. It is, however, she who shoulders the necessity, when others, notably her sister Ismene, do not. But Knox is right that there is no doubt in her mind: right from the beginning of the play Antigone makes it clear that she is going to ignore the decree and bury her brother. This is her conception of her duty and her intention, and she simply brushes away with contempt Ismene's dithering and eventual conformity to the law and to the rights of the city. For Hegel we have here the three-step of thesis and antithesis—the two conflicting moral principles—leading to catastrophe (Antigone is executed and Creon's wife and son die as well), and so needing a resolution and synthesis, presumably in a more nuanced balance between private and civic duty.

Antigone is certainly heroic, and even ferocious, but there is also that tincture of willfulness, or blindness, albeit one that leaves the audience sufficiently on her side to appreciate the full depth of her tragedy. Sophocles characteristically explores this structure, for similar reservations surround Oedipus, whose single-minded, intransigent quest to unravel the issue of his identity precipitates his tragedy, or Philoctetes, who is bitterly adamant that he will not help the Greeks who have abandoned him on Lemnos, although it is prophesied that without his help they will be unable to take Troy (it is true that at the end of the play, after divine intervention, Philoctetes relents, but the moral drama happens before that).

We might already see some reason to qualify Hegel's account, since while Antigone can be said to be activated by a single, objective moral principle, this is not so evidently true of either Oedipus or Philoctetes. However, the single-mindedness is certainly there, and since tragedy requires conflict, Sophocles has to create external conflict that therefore is situated between the hero and his integrity (or willfulness) on the one hand and opposing outside forces on the other. Hegel was certainly right to emphasize the contrast when we turn to Shakespeare. Here the tragedy centers around a figure who is far from single-minded, blind, or obsessed. The great Victorian critic A. C. Bradley identified the difference decisively:

> The truth is, that the type of tragedy in which the hero opposes to a hostile force an undivided soul, is not the Shakespearean type. The souls of those who contend with the hero may be thus undivided; they generally are; but, as a rule, the hero, though he pursues his fated way, is, at least at some point in the action, and sometimes at many, torn by an inward struggle; and it is frequently at such points that Shakespeare shows his most extraordinary power. If further we compare the earlier tragedies with the later, we find that it is in the latter, the maturest works, that this inward struggle is most emphasized. In the last of them, *Coriolanus*, its interest completely eclipses toward the close of the play that of the outward conflict. *Romeo and Juliet, Richard III, Richard II*, where the hero contends with an outward force, but comparatively little with himself, are all early plays.
>
> If we are to include the outer and the inner struggle in a conception more definite than that of conflict in general, we must employ some such phrase as "spiritual force." This will mean whatever forces act in the human spirit, whether good or evil, whether personal passion or impersonal principle; doubts, desires, scruples, ideas—whatever can animate, shake, possess, and drive a man's soul.[5]

Macbeth, Othello, Lear, Anthony, Coriolanus, and Hamlet all face inner conflict, doubt, and struggle. It is, however, inadequate to describe the torn hero, as Hegel does, as simply idiosyncratic, an arbitrary constellation of subjective personality traits. The different voices contending in the hero are just as clearly moral voices as they are in Oedipus or Philoctetes. Hamlet, for instance, can be said to put on the yoke of necessity just as much as Agamemnon or Antigone, even if the necessity is not conceptualized in terms of the command of the gods but in terms of an inner compulsion. The struggle is also quite consistent, as Bradley notices, with the eventual emergence of a decision, so that the tragedy unfolds from what he nicely calls "a fatal tendency to identify the whole being with one interest, object, passion, or habit of mind." The problem is precisely that the hero suppresses some aspect of himself in favor of this tendency, and runs upon ruin by so doing. If this tendency is thought of as the emergence of a kind of integrity from what was previously divided and conflicted, then it has to be seen as a fall rather than an ascent, a disaster rather than a blessing.

Shakespeare, of course, did not invent the conflicted character. It can be traced at least as far back as Euripides and is ever-present in Ovid (the very idea of metamorphosis implies the existence of forces disposing us to change). Psychomachia, or inner struggle, is endemic to the religious condition. And the same is true not only of Shakespeare's heroes but also his villains. In his poem *The Rape of Lucrece*, the rapist Tarquin, already bent on his appalling crime, puts the case against what he is doing quite admirably:

> "What win I, if I gain the thing I seek?
> A dream, a breath, a froth of fleeting joy.
> Who buys a minute's mirth to wail a week?
> Or sells eternity to get a toy?
> For one sweet grape who will the vine destroy?

> Or what fond beggar, but to touch the crown,
> Would with the sceptre straight be strucken down? . . ."

And it is not just fear of the consequences that haunts him, for he also knows that if he proceeds, he will never be able to trust himself, or anyone else, again. It will be the collapse of his own foundations, as indeed it proves to be, and succumbing to temptation is often just that.

There are normal times when it is wholly admirable to be steadfast, resolute, unconflicted, and therefore when integrity is unmistakably a virtue. The person of integrity knows what to do, and does it. But as we have been exploring, there are also times when certainty and single-mindedness indicate something less admirable: a deafness to voices that should be heard or a blindness to aspects of a situation that need to be considered. Do similar complexities affect our two other virtues: sincerity and authenticity?

The literary critic Lionel Trilling made a famous and influential distinction between this pair.[6] He associated the rise of sincerity as a concern in the early modern period with the breakdown of medieval, feudal structures within which people had found themselves in static, small-scale, well-understood worlds. The new world of cities and commerce, and shifting populations, brought with it an anxiety about whether people were what they seemed to be or claimed to be. Trust is more secure when we have ongoing, repeated interactions with a small number of relatively permanent friends or neighbors. It is much less secure when people's identities are obscured, or transactions are one-off, or it is impossible to mobilize social sanctions against the transgressors. If duplicity and disguise are the dangers, then it is understandable that sincerity, a straightforward correspondence between who you are and what you present to others, or between how you think and what you say, becomes all the more prized, and its presence or absence becomes a major topic in the literature of the time (perhaps it is due to become so in ours, when the possibility of fraud on the web is so alarming).

Ordinary honesty is not, however, a very exciting ideal. Calling someone an "honest fellow," rather like calling a man a decent chap, has a patronizing ring to it, while an "honest woman" does not even have to be particularly free of guile.[7] Authenticity, on the other hand, is more of an achievement. In Hegelian terms it comes about when self-consciousness has achieved a higher stage than that of simple individualism. Sincerity is merely a tool for providing reliable and useful interactions between individuals. Authenticity, however, is not merely a correspondence between inner thought and outward expression, although it implies at least that much. It requires in addition an achievement within the self. It requires deep self-knowledge or deep self-awareness, coupled with a determination to express that self in choices, actions, inclinations, or feelings. Its enemy is self-deception or misunderstanding, a split between our "deepest" selves and the way we think we are or describe ourselves as being, even to ourselves. If its first commandment is, again, the Delphic inscription "know thyself," then its second would be the injunction to be yourself.

In Hegel's *Phenomenology of Spirit*, authenticity arrives as an ideal a stage after the ideal of self-direction under the yoke of reason, or, in other words, obedience to the objective moral law. As we have seen, rational agency in the Kantian exposition is just this ability to subserve one's interests to the objective and impersonal moral law: the categorical imperative. The Romantic rebellion against this tyranny looked for a different, personal source of moral strength and found it in the innermost drives or ways of being of the individual agent. It is as if we substitute the Byronic hero for the dutiful hausfrau. With this romantic rebellion comes the idea of the "genius," the hero or artist whose innermost self is different from that of other people, but which dictates what the individual *must* do, with all the authority that, in Kant, attaches to the moral law itself. It is perhaps a testimony to the magnetism of this idea that influential modern interpretations of Kant in effect dress him in this Romantic clothing, reinterpreting the authority of the categorical imperative as nothing more than the efflorescence of an acte gratuit, an arbitrary choice of the authentic self-governing individual.[8] But we have already cast doubt on this entirely un-Hegelian, un-Kantian, and indeed rather odd suggestion.

In the existentialist tradition, from Kierkegaard to Heidegger and Sartre, authenticity means a permanent freedom (coupled with a parallel responsibility) to take control of who one is, and to be prepared to reject the conventional scripts foisted on one from outside. It implies standing at an angle to the "inauthentic" lives we feel forced into by the modern world, and standing ready to break free from the categories it imposes upon us. The idea is, of course, especially appealing in oppressive social and political situations. A desire to escape the script society writes for you that prescribes how to comport yourself as, say, a Jew, or a woman, or an immigrant, may be not only understandable but entirely admirable.

However, the best-ever piece of light verse about a philosopher introduces a doubt about authenticity, in the exacting double-dactyl form:

Higgledy-piggledy
Herr Rektor Heidegger

Said to his students
To Being be True

Lest you should fall into
Inauthenticity
This I believe—
And the Führer does too!

The verses suggest there is something fake about Heidegger's injunctions to authenticity, and it is easy to sympathize. Indeed, Theodor Adorno wrote a whole book (*The Jargon of Authenticity*) attacking him on the topic, without managing to put it quite so neatly as the verses do. But authenticity certainly has its jargon—wholeness, again, integrity, truth, the natural, the self-sufficient, the real, the original, the rooted, all favorably contrasted with what is superficial, artificial, imposed, merely conventional, social, constructed, fragmented, self-estranged, false.

If we return to the worries about the self that we voiced in chapter 1, we may become puzzled about authenticity. Of course, in moments of disenchantment, there is consolation to be had imagining a Real Me, a butterfly escaped from the chrysalis of the social and the conventional, a self untrammeled by the artificial restrictions of society, beautifully free from the sleepwalking and the mechanical drudgery of modern life. The Everyday Me is repetitive, confined by its role or roles, bourgeois and cautious, timid and prudent. The Real Me is a very different kettle of fish, most likely contemptuous of restraint, free, wild, romantic, courageous, creative. As Nietzsche puts it, the one is a camel, patiently bearing the social luggage placed upon it, but the other is surely a lion.

As soon as it is put like that, however, the fantasy begins to dissolve. Why on earth should the Real Me be a lion, or even a butterfly? Presumably, it is more likely to be a human being, having grown in the way that human beings do, for instance, by imitating others, or coming to speak a mother tongue, by being protected and encouraged, guided and trained, and by such processes alone coming to bear an enormous cultural and social baggage. It is not likely to be all that creative or romantic if it can't speak, and it is not possible for it to be entirely independent of society if it can. As we saw when discussing Collingwood in chapter 1, perhaps it cannot even be a self-conscious person without this social support. Admittedly, William Blake's or Wordsworth's celebration of childhood evades this problem by presenting the prelinguistic infant as a happy blend of innocence and integrity. But this is hardly a consoling fantasy for most of us. We want to imagine our Real Selves doing better than babbling.

Walter Mitty thought that the real Walter Mitty was a Hollywood hero, fearlessly commanding great machines and great enterprises. He was wrong. The real Walter Mitty was Walter Mitty, hopelessly imagining being what he foolishly imagined a hero to be, as an escape from the humdrum way he actually lived. His fantasies are inevitably no better than he is, as is sufficiently indicated by mention of Hollywood. The blueprints of authenticity are themselves fakes. This may be obvious in Walter Mitty's case, but he is all of us, and if we escape his fantasies, it will only be to fall victim to more insidious ones. Our imaginings may dwell on authentic country living, or authentic adventure, but be similarly infected by the fake and constructed scripts of the heritage industry or the travel brochure. Authentic country living means modern conveniences and wine delivered to the door, while authentic adventure needs a guide and an insurance policy. If we love our classics, our heroes may be a degree more sophisticated than Mitty's, but even Homer's heroes are actors, and their scripts are myths. Plato may have been wrong to banish the artists, but given what they supply us for fantasy and daydreams, he was not foolish.[9]

To this it may reasonably be replied that we should not expect real authenticity to show itself in people's own daydreams. The Romantic view is that only the rare Byronic genius has a real self, while many traditions in philosophy, from before Plato through Christianity to Freud, have insisted that the True Self lies only at the end of a long quest, a hard process of analysis, discovery, and purification. And while we should all put our hands up in favor of processes of self-examination and self-improvement, we may more reasonably question whether such processes result in discovery of some authentic self that was there all along, or whether they give us only the construction of a new way to act, a new script to follow, or a new persona to put on. The metaphor of being born again may be more accurate than it sounds, for there is never a guarantee that what is newly born will be less self-deceived, less of a bore or an idiot, or in any admirable sense more "authentic" than whoever started the process. It is not usually enviable to have friends and spouses who go in for self-help manuals, or put a lot of store by realizing their true natures. The quest for the True Self can lead to silence, prayer, psychoanalysis, or Zen meditation, but it can also lead to drink, drugs, and despair.

Strangely enough, authenticity was a particular watchword of existentialism. Yet the idea that "existence precedes essence" is precisely the idea that there is no True or Real Me, and certainly not one masked and only dimly visible under the gray paint of civilization. The existentialists were thus far good Hegelians, profoundly mistrusting the self-sufficiency of the True Self, insisting that the self is always the product of community and of social recognition by others. Hegel saw this recognition in terms of restless competition and conflict, and Sartre thought it made life itself hellish, having as he did a particularly dim view of other people. But now there is a problem, because authenticity in the sense suggested so far could not survive without the notion of the antecedent True Self. So for existentialism, it needed to become reconfigured, not any longer as congruence with an original, natural self but as pure autonomy, or the conscious seizure of freedom and choice. Inauthentic living or living in bad faith imply denying the omnipresence of choice. By contrast, the truly authentic seize it and thereby take responsibility for their lives. When Sartre propounded the famous paradox that the French were never so free as under the German occupation, he meant that the occupation forced awareness of choice on everyone, however they then responded to it.

However, Sartre only half-escaped the tyranny of the Real Self. Suspiciously, the authentic life turned out to be not only one lived in awareness of choice but one in which the response to that awareness followed a definite direction: anarchic, Bohemian, suffused with hatred of the bourgeoisie, sexually unconventional, and volubly left-wing. Just as the word "faith" only retains its positive connotations when your faith coincides with mine—otherwise being dogmatism or lunacy—so the words "authentic choice" only functioned to introduce ideals when they meant the same kind of choices as Sartre's own. Otherwise, the injunction to live in awareness of choice becomes disappointingly empty, even more so than Heidegger's dismal injunction to live in awareness of Death. Perhaps Sartre forgot that people might choose to be bourgeois and conventional, cautious, monogamous, and conservative, with every bit as much awareness as any antihero enthusiast for the Bohemian life of the café. Indeed, Kant believed that for rational agents, there was no escaping the burden of reflection and judgment, so that a pure "wanton," unself-consciously following desire without ever subjecting it to the reflection of self-consciousness, is not a bad or unenlightened kind of person, let alone a Noble Savage, but not a person at all. Sartre's injunction is then empty, since people are bound to be following it, however they then behave.

As a psychologist Sartre gave marvelous vignettes of persons trying to conceal their own complicity in events from themselves, such as the girl who let her hand become a "thing" in order to duck responsibility, and to appear neither to encourage nor discourage the advances of the lover.[10] But this too will have been an exercise of freedom, a cunning strategy admirably adapted to her circumstance, and the only aspect worth calling bad faith would be any later disclaimer of knowledge of what she was doing. Sartre can also write of people who prefer not to think of some options as open to them. But he misleads us if he suggests that this is always a failing. It is the path of virtue to regard some options as closed. With sufficient years behind me, I live my life ignoring tightrope walking as a live option, but far from this being a failing, it is no doubt a matter of some relief to my wife and children. It is just not true that you should try every experience once, except incest and folk-dancing.

If Real Selves and Self-Realization are fantasies, and choice is not a specific value worth enjoining, then there is not much left to the notion of authenticity. But if it is so easy to mock, what explains its continued currency, and what purposes does it serve? One function is to fill the vacuum left by the death of God. If Kantian universal objectivity has failed us, and if values and norms have no source in the supernatural world, where else can they be grounded? Authentic commitment, self-legislation of values and ideals, are appealing substitutes for external authority and command. Obedience only to the dictates of the heart substitutes for the discredited authority of gods and their interpreters. Morality becomes no more than an exercise in autonomy or self-government, a matter of truth to the inner determinations of the self.

Trilling cited Polonius's otherwise banal advice to his departing son Laertes as the first expression of the idea: "To thine own self be true, and it must follow as the night the day, thou canst not then to any man be false." Fine words, but Shakespeare is carefully putting them into the mouth of the thoroughly ordinary and unimaginative busybody Polonius. And why should we believe them? Think instead of the contradictory and fragmented self of modernism, the self-conscious self that we have seen Shakespeare himself exploring. What if Laertes' own self is insincere and insecure, irresolute and unknowing, all the way down? If this is how he is, and Laertes expresses his own self, he might give promises he cannot keep, begin undertakings he cannot follow through, use language that means nothing or implies what is not true, and say things about which he is self-deceived, and just because he would most like them to be true. Even worse, Laertes's own self might be steeped in sin. "Get in touch with your inner self," urges the therapist, perhaps unconscious that the inner self may be a pretty nasty piece of work (Bernard Williams once invited us to reflect on quite how awful it might be if people followed the similar injunction to be a man). The Real Selves of our prominent politicians are exactly as they manifest themselves as being: tricksy, dishonest, self-serving, and, to cap it all, usually in denial about their own corruptions.

Did Polonius then have some guarantee of pure gold underneath the base alloys that make up the empirical self? Perhaps he was abetted by the rise of inner-light Protestantism, with conscience standing inside as an unmistakable guide, the candle of the Lord, or the voice that must be heard. To be deaf to it implies being willfully deaf. A related idea of virtue as integrity, harmony, or wholeness is at least as old as Plato. In Plato, however, the harmonious self is something to be worked for, an achievement only attainable by the wise and the just. As with the Romantic genius, these will be the select few whose natures have the gold within them from the beginning. But even they will also need to have undergone the most extraordinary upbringing and rigid education. Nobody can become wise and just simply by listening to their deepest inner voice. Virtue is not the birthright of every man, or every man uncorrupted by insidious external influences. It took what Nietzsche saw as the sentimental, democratic, feminine touch of Christianity to add that story.

But perhaps we cannot shake off Protestantism so easily. We certainly find it difficult to believe that anyone could write the kinds of stuff or say the kinds of thing that we routinely hear from public figures without at some level squirming at their own lack of integrity. We think there must be an inner candle somewhere, however much the subject has tried to hide from its light. If they allowed themselves to look at their sins, we think, they would doubtless repent. Surely it cannot be baseness or fragmentation all the way down. But perhaps we are wrong, and perhaps it is.

This suggests a second reason we cling to authenticity, which is that we feel we need it to underwrite sincerity, the easier notion that we certainly need. As we have seen, this ought to be a much easier notion than authenticity. We can identify lapses from simple honesty without tying ourselves up in images of the inner self. Saying that a thing is so when you believe it is not is often simple enough, detectable, a cause of resentment and rejection in others, and if the deception is fraudulent, this may be provable in a court of law. Searching for a True Self or hoping to express a True Self by contrast are, as we have been exploring, at best fraught and at worst entering a wild-goose chase. Yet the two are connected in subtle ways, perhaps indicated by the thought that sincerity could not sustain the value we put on it without some help from a lurking conception of authenticity.

The idea is that sincerity is not a secure achievement, attainable at a lower Hegelian level of being than authenticity, which only comes about when humanity has reached a higher level of consciousness. It is rather that real sincerity is impossible, or if we prefer it, what substitutes for sincerity is too cheap to value highly, if there is no such thing as authenticity in the self. Thus, if all the world's a stage, you cannot expect consistency from the world any more than you can expect it from actors in their professional roles. You should not, for instance, expect fidelity or loyalty to a previous part, for the persona who breaks the promise is most likely not the persona who gave it. You should not expect the sentiment sincerely felt and voiced at one time to be an accurate indicator of the sentiment that will be just as sincerely felt and voiced at another. The selves it is appropriate or strategic to present at each moment are not linked by ties of identity. They make up only an agglomeration or a commonwealth, and any loyalties through time are at best the fortunate precipitate from favorable social circumstances. Even when faced with the most blatant chicanery or abject disgrace, well, hey, we just need to draw a line under it and move on. Cheap intensity of expression and conviction of the moment substitute for wholeness of character. And people in general become like their politicians, men without inner light, men without qualities. In fact, our world becomes a world of players, but it is a mistake, portentously christened the "fundamental attribution error" in social psychology, to suppose that anybody actually has a character. The writer Robert Musil put the fear that faces all of us in his description of the man without qualities, the protagonist of his book:

> And now just run your mind over the sort of man he is. He always knows what to do. He can gaze into a woman's eyes. He can exercise his intelligence efficiently on any given problem at any given moment. He can box. He is talented, strong-willed, unprejudiced, he has courage and endurance, he can go at things with a dash and he can be cool and cautious—I have no intention of examining all this in detail, let him have all these qualities! For in the end he hasn't got them at all! They have made him what he is, they have set his course for him, and yet they don't belong to him. When he is angry, something in him laughs. When he is sad, he is up to something. When he is moved by something, he will reject it. Every bad action will seem good to him in some connection or other. And it will always be only a possible context that will decide what he thinks of a thing. Nothing is stable for him. Everything is fluctuating, part of a whole, among innumerable wholes that presumably are part of a super-whole, which, however, he doesn't know the slightest thing about. So every one of his answers is a part-answer, every one of his feelings only a point of view, and whatever a thing is, it doesn't matter to him what it is, it's only some accompanying "way in which it is," some addition or other which matters to him.[11]

Hume, and the Buddhist anatta tradition, may suggest that the man without qualities is all of us, rather than the casualty and the emblem of a particular time and place. Lost, uprooted, "unable to take his own side in an argument," he is certainly recognizable.

Nevertheless, we want to recoil from the ghastly picture of human life this offers. If this is the alternative, we think, then the pendulum had better swing back to real, true, inner selves. But as so often, the right way forward may be to reject both alternatives. We do not have to fantasize an inner John Wayne in order to escape an inner George Bush or Tony Blair. If we are ordinarily fortunate, we have sufficient defenses built by the world's own processes of education, upbringing, and experience, the ones that made us what we are. We do indeed have real selves, and it is to be hoped that many of them show us to be sincere in our doings, and across a wide spectrum of everyday interactions, wholeheartedly virtuous. But these selves are not inner, and not overlaid and concealed by the contingent circumstances that in fact created them. They are our empirical selves, with their empirical constancies, sometimes our empirical contradictions, and often our empirical complexities. This was the moral we took from Joyce's wholly adequate, complete depiction of Leopold Bloom.

We can indeed wonder about possibilities of improvement, and dwell on ideals of virtue and excellence as aids to it. Even Plato allowed this function to the artists. We can undertake self-examination, although the term is often misplaced. For when we ask ourselves what we really want, or what we really believe about something, and find the question hard, this is not because for once we cannot find ourselves or cannot interpret what we find. The question is not answered by uncovering an inner, preformed self with an unambiguous desire or belief. It is answered by looking one more time at the choice or at the evidence and deciding what to desire or what to believe. It is not navel-gazing that gives us such solutions but thinking the thing through one more time, in engagement with the world. It is not an exercise of discovery but what Kant would have called an exercise of freedom: the pursuit of opinion by mobilizing evidence and reasons. Here "I do not know what I think about Schubert," for instance, really means "I do not know what to think about Schubert," and that would be answered not by further acquaintance with one's inner self but by further acquaintance with Schubert's works. "I don't know whether I want to go to Disneyworld" is a practical problem, to be solved (if it needs solving) by thinking one more time about the likely costs and benefits of such a visit. There need be nothing inauthentic about being in the dilemma, and nothing inauthentic either about the fact that some features of such a visit will strike you as costs and others will attract you as benefits. You may be the victim of cunning advertising, conventional manipulations, false images, or groundless fears as you think of these things, but that is just bad luck. You would then be an authentic victim.

An authentic Vermeer is a real Vermeer, or, if you like, just a Vermeer, as opposed to a fake or substitute Vermeer. An inauthentic Vermeer is a fake or copy, perhaps masquerading as a Vermeer. Similarly, the authentic Walter Mitty was Walter Mitty. James Joyce gave us the authentic Leopold Bloom, whose authentic nature is manifested in the myriad of small things his little odyssey put in his way.

9
Envoi

The picture I have had to paint is not straightforward. Perhaps surprisingly, given the weight of moralistic writing about these topics, there is no simple, bumper sticker–sized philosophical or moral conclusion to be drawn. But the complexity is itself instructive. We have seen things that are good, such as proper pride in our own achievements, fade into those that are bad, such as Rousseau's amour propre. We have seen too that proper pride implicitly involves comparison with the average or the commonplace, so that Rousseau's own ideal of life without comparisons is itself doubtful. Meanwhile, a tincture of vanity itself is in order where it shades into simply keeping up appearances, or is only the perhaps faltering attempt to ensure a reception for an individual in the social world. It is even in order when allied with sympathy, so the tribute it expects from others is a tribute it is also prepared to pay to them. It is out of order when this is not so, and it becomes overbearing, self-obsessing, or arrogant. Similarly, pride is in order when it consorts with the need to do something well, or not to let oneself down or to deliver less than one's best. It is out of order when it becomes hubristic, or fertilizes a belief in one's right to transcend the obligations, duties, or hesitations that beset others. Self-esteem is in order when it implies a just appreciation of one's genuine abilities, but it too means taking a proper place alongside others in the social world, and it is out of order when it becomes tainted with the excesses of confidence, conceit, or the perception of a right to demand more from others than it is prepared to offer to them. So in all these things, as Aristotle would have said, there is a balance to be struck, a mean to be found, and it may be a mean between more than one extreme and another. Competing ideals and interests may forever tug us toward places we should not be. And even Aristotle's metaphor of the balance and the mean may be too simple, for finding the right mixture of these attitudes, emotions, or stances toward the self may be like finding the center of gravity of a cloud. But it should not be disappointing that there are no one-word commandments, for we have been dealing with the complex matter of positioning oneself among others in the social world. And neither we ourselves, nor the others, nor the context and the forces that push us and attract us are simple.

In spite of this complexity, we have also explored cases where things are obviously out of hand. The monstrous excesses of the "greed is good" culture that spread across banks and boardrooms in the last thirty years find no defenses here. Kleptoparasitism is ugly wherever it is found, and exposing some of the self-deceptions that underlie it and, in the eyes of the wealthy, justify it, is not the least important job for philosophy and psychology, responsive, we may hope, to the great myths of our history. Narcissus, Midas, and the myth of the Fall may tell us a great deal of what we need to know, while the sad lives of men and women in thrall to the blandishments of the various industries that prey upon vanity should be an awful warning to all of us.

What is to be done about these things? If avarice is built into human nature, not much. But if the "greed is good" world was, as I have described, largely a cultural construction that supplanted any sense of civic society, public service, or common decency in the last third of the twentieth century, then a reverse shift should be possible, even if all the powers of hell, from Gordon Gekko to Rupert Murdoch and downward, oppose it. Certainly, it was easier to let the evil genie out of the bottle than it will be to put it back in. But bit by bit, with people working in schools, in media, by example, and over time, the ideological climate can shift. It should not be too difficult to suggest to children that Narcissus's only companion is Echo, and at the end there was nothing left. The great economist John Maynard Keynes, always wonderfully alert to the climate of ideas or cloud of misunderstandings that surround economics itself, said that "soon or late it is ideas, not vested interests, which are dangerous for good or evil."[1] His contrast, however, is a little simplistic, since the vested interests are very good at controlling which ideas are promoted and blazoned forth, drumming into people that most depressing of political lies: TINA—There Is No Alternative. But there is.

So after all this, can you look in the mirror? Are you worth it? Certainly. One of your virtues is that you would not have read this far without an interest in moral issues, pride, self-respect, esteem, and their blacker shadows of vanity, envy, narcissism, and insensitivity. That interest is itself a moral credit to you. And in any case, you are certainly worth it to the same extent as anyone else, sharing a common humanity, with its ups and downs, virtues and vices, bright spots and dark shadows. You have the voice within your breast representing Smith's impartial spectator without, the voice of conscience, and at your best you might even listen to it. You can even pamper yourself as you deserve, by cultivating an awareness of the world around you and the people in it and having attainable goals that measure your success in dealing with it. It is cheaper than buying vanities, but more productive of real happiness. Or as the seventeenth-century mystical poet Thomas Traherne put it:

> You never enjoy the world aright, till the Sea itself floweth in your veins, till you are clothed with the heavens, and crowned with the stars: and perceive yourself to be the sole heir of the whole world, and more than so, because men are in it who are every one sole heirs as well as you.[2]

You do not have to be an iron man, and you do not have to be ashamed of proper pride and self-regard. And even if you think you bestride the narrow world like a colossus, you are the creation of luck, not immune to time and chance, and any day infirmity or accident can find you, depending entirely on the good offices of others.

Smith thought that our tendency to admire the rich or the great, instead of the virtuous and the useful, was "the great and most universal cause of the corruption of our moral sentiments." I do not promise that this little tour of these landscapes will cure this corruption. It takes more than a single voice to oppose an ideology, and all the forces ranged behind the lie that there is no alternative. But the tour might pit against it some awareness of what we are doing, and the pitfalls that surround doing it, so I think it is unlikely to do us any harm.

Notes

The works of Adam Smith, David Hume, and Immanuel Kant have specific reference requirements. Citing publication and page number can be less useful than giving the other way of referring to passages such as book, part, section, chapter (e.g., *Treatise* 1.2.3, 4.), or in the case of Kant, the number of volume in the Prussian Academy edition of his works, followed by paragraph number (e.g., 4:631). These free the reader from needing the same edition that I used. However, for Hume, Kant, and Smith, I have also put in specific editions and page numbers.

INTRODUCTION

1. Immanuel Kant, *Anthropology from a Pragmatic Point of View*, ed. Robert B. Louden (Cambridge: Cambridge University Press, 2006), preface, 3, 7.119.

2. David Hume, "Of the Standard of Taste," in *Essays: Moral, Political, and Literary,* ed. E. Miller (Indianapolis: Liberty Press, 1987), part 1, essay 23; hereafter *Essays.* Hume goes on to point out that while we

agree about the generalities, when it comes to applications and particular cases, cracks soon open up.

3. Owen Chadwick, *John Cassian: A Study in Primitive Monasticism* (Cambridge: Cambridge University Press, 1950), 95.

4. *Handlyng Synne* (1301), by Robert de Brunne, is one of the more appealing.

5. Immanuel Kant, *The Metaphysics of Morals*, trans. and ed. Mary Gregor (Cambridge: Cambridge University Press, 1996), 167, 6:409; italics in original.

6. It is no accident that this obsession coincided with the rise in the West, of economic models of rational activity, and the annihilation of any notion of civil and public virtue; see also chapter 6.

7. John Bunyan, *The Pilgrim's Progress* (Oxford: World's Classics, 1966), 86.

8. Bertrand Russell, *A History of Western Philosophy* (London: Unwin, 1984), 191.

9. Thomas Hobbes, *Leviathan*, ed. Richard Tuck (Cambridge: Cambridge University Press, 1996), 1:11, 70.

10. Kant gives different formulations of the famous categorical imperative, which I discuss below. He is particularly hard on desire and inclination in *The Critique of Practical Reason* (trans. Werner S. Pluhar [Indianapolis: Hackett, 2002], 150, 5:118), but it is dangerous to take such a passage out of context.

11. Rae Langton, "Duty and Desolation," *Philosophy* 67 (1992): 481–505.

12. The imperative commands us to act only upon maxims that we can will to be universalized, that is, such that everyone acts on them (see chapters 6 and 7). As Langton shows, there is room for debate about whether it actually obliged Maria von Herbert to be as open about her history as she was.

13. It is difficult for a layman reading about the side effects of these drugs to have any grasp of why they are indeed widely prescribed, especially as for anything but very severe depression they offer little or no advantage over placebos. And since for severe depression drugs that enhance as opposed to inhibiting serotonin reuptake also work, the science seems at best speculative, or actually quite at sea. Yet there are

around fifty million prescriptions for these in one year in the UK alone: nearly one for each inhabitant. (For more on psychotropic drugs, see below, chapter 6).

14. Hume, "The Epicurean," in *Essays*, part 1, essay 15.

15. Which chimes in with Kant as well, although his concept of self-mastery is one of obedience to the moral law, which we discuss later.

16. W. E. Henley, "Invictus." Literary critics will divide over whether the awful circumstances in which the poem was written excuse its combination of desperation and bravado.

17. One of the best known is by James Stockdale, who became a prisoner of the North Vietnamese for seven years and survived partly by internalizing the philosophy of Epictetus. *Thoughts of a Philosophical Fighter Pilot* (Stanford, CA: Hoover Institution Press, 1995). A fictional version is given in Tom Wolfe's novel *A Man in Full* (London: Jonathan Cape, 1998).

18. Michel de Montaigne, "Vanity," in *Essays*, in *The Complete Works of Montaigne*, trans. Donald M. Frame (Stanford, CA: Stanford University Press, 1967), 766.

CHAPTER I
THE SELF

1. Iris Murdoch, *The Sovereignty of Good* (London: Routledge & Kegan Paul, 1970), 91.

2. Ibid., 103.

3. Ibid., 86.

4. John Carey, *What Good Are the Arts?* (London: Faber & Faber, 2005), 41.

5. This case is well made by Richard Moran in "Iris Murdoch and Existentialism," in *Iris Murdoch, Philosopher*, ed. Justin Broackes (Oxford: Oxford University Press, 2012).

6. Immanuel Kant, *Critique of Pure Reason*, trans. Norman Kemp Smith (London: Macmillan 1963), 139, A112.

7. Quoted in Nancy Sherman, *Stoic Warriors* (Oxford: Oxford University Press, 2005), 165.

8. David Hume, *A Treatise of Human Nature*, ed. L. A. Selby-Bigge (Oxford: Oxford University Press, 1888), 1.4.6, 252; hereafter *Treatise*. I have slightly modernized Selby-Bigge's translation in citations from this edition.

9. They include Derek Parfit, *Reasons and Persons* (Oxford: Oxford University Press, 1984), and with very different, intricate, and ambitious arguments, Mark Johnston, *Surviving Death* (Princeton: Princeton University Press, 2010, esp. chapter 3). Johnston quotes with approval Mill's idea that we live on "in the onward rush of mankind." But as Woody Allen nearly said, "I don't want to live on in the onward rush of mankind. I want to live on in my apartment."

10. The example of sakes is due to W. V. Quine.

11. This kind of approach is associated with the philosopher Daniel Dennett. See, for instance, his *Brainstorms* (Cambridge, MA: MIT Press, 1981).

12. L. Wittgenstein, *Tractatus Logico-Philosophicus*, trans. D. F. Pears and B. F. McGuinness (London: Routledge & Kegan Paul 1963), 5.631.

13. Ibid., 5.631 and 5.64.

14. Ibid., 6.431.

15. Ibid.

16. Lewis Carroll, *Alice Through the Looking Glass*, chapter 4.

17. Or so Carroll tells us. But the biography of Alice Liddell seems to bear it out.

18. However, Bounderby's vice is not unusual. Monty Python's classic "Four Yorkshiremen" sketch, easily available on YouTube, is built on the same all-too-recognizable characteristics.

19. Gwen Raverat, *Period Piece* (London: Faber, 1952), 176.

20. Hume, *Treatise*, 3.3.1, 589.

21. Kant is surprisingly relaxed about such social elasticity, in spite of his notorious denunciations of any kind of lies. The difference seems to be that in social interactions, it is generally understood that sincerity is not expected, so the "lie" is more like a ritual or pretense, or a piece of playacting. It therefore does not deny the recipient the ability to use his or her own reason to the full.

22. R. G. Collingwood, *Principles of Art* (Oxford: Oxford University Press, 1938), 248.

CHAPTER 2
LIRIOPE'S SON

1. Ovid, *Metamorphoses*, book 3.61. All quotations are from the translation by A. D. Melville (Oxford: Oxford World Classics, 1986).

2. It is a sad curiosity that my generation was reared on *The Greek Myths* by Robert Graves, an enormously successful, two-volume Penguin book. Yet Graves offered no interpretation or insight into the myths he recounted. Half a century after Freud, he told them as if he were reciting a long, dull telephone directory.

3. The film of that name is directed by Sofia Coppola.

4. Adam Smith, *The Theory of Moral Sentiments*, ed. D. D. Raphael and A. L. Macfie, vol. 1 of the Glasgow Edition of the Works and Correspondence of Adam Smith (Indianapolis: Liberty Fund, 1982), 1.3.2, 22; 125; hereafter *Theory*.

CHAPTER 3
WORTH IT?

1. Ibid., 1.3.2, 1; 51.

2. Ibid., 50.

3. In 2012, L'Oréal made profits of €2.87bn ($5.1 billion) on sales of €22.46bn ($30.2 billion).

4. Jessica Bennett, *Newsweek*, July 2010, http://www.thedailybeast.com/newsweek/2010/07/19/the-beauty-advantage.html.

5. Plato, *Gorgias*, lines 463–65.

6. Erasmus, *The Praise of Folly*, trans. Clarence H. Miller (New Haven: Yale University Press, 1979), 70.

7. Jean-Jacques Rousseau, *Émile*, trans. Barbara Foxley (London: Everyman Books, 1972), 347.

CHAPTER 4
HUBRIS AND THE FRAGILE SELF

1. Carolyn C. Morf and Frederick Rhodewalt, "Unravelling the Paradoxes of Narcissism," *Psychological Inquiry* 12, no. 4 (2001): 178.

2. Alan Bennett, *Smut* (London: Faber & Faber, 2010), 116.

3. David Owen, *The Hubris Syndrome* (London: Politico's Publishing, 2007), 1–2.

4. Isaiah, 14:13.

5. Of course, this doctrine of Augustine's was controversial from the beginning. A hostile contemporary monk, Saint Vincent, summed it up as: "God has created the greater part of the human race for eternal damnation; God is the author of our sins; adulteries, incests and murders happen because God has decreed them; repentance is useless for anyone predestined for death; when most Christians pray 'thy will be done' they are praying for their own destruction, since this is the will of God." In other words, Augustine is so afraid of pride that he wants to destroy any human excuse for pride, and therefore attacks free will and human responsibility, but by doing so risks leaving God as the author of our worst sins. We see Milton facing this conundrum below; Hume is naturally quietly gleeful about it (*Enquiry Concerning Human Understanding*, ed. Tom L. Beauchamp [Oxford: Oxford University Press, 2000], 164, para. 36).

6. Belinda Jane Board and Katarina Fritzon, "Disordered Personalities at Work," *Psychology, Crime and Law* 11, no. 1 (March 2005): 17–32.

7. Smith, *Theory*, 2.3.1, 6; 96.

8. Rousseau, *Émile*, 260.

9. Smith, *Theory*, 1.3.3, 8; 65.

10. Saint Gregory, *Morals on the Book of Job*, vol. 3, ed. John Henry Parker, J.G.F. Rivington, and J. Rivington (London, 1844), book 34, section 52, 657.

CHAPTER 5
SELF-ESTEEM, AMOUR PROPRE, PRIDE

1. Roy F. Baumeister, Jennifer D. Campbell, Joachim I. Krueger, and Kathleen D. Vohs, "Does High Self-Esteem Cause Better Performance, Interpersonal Success, Happiness, or Healthier Lifestyles?," *Psychological Science in the Public Interest* 4, no. 1 (May 2003).

2. This section is indebted to chapter 17 of *Irrationality*, by Stuart Sutherland (London: Pinter & Martin, 2007).

3. Smith, *Theory*, 1.3.3, 5; 63.

4. Jean-Jacques Rousseau, *A Discourse on the Moral Effects of the Arts and Sciences*, ed. G.D.H. Cole (London: J. M. Dent, 1973), 14.

5. Montaigne, "Of Vanity," in *Complete Works*, ed. Frame, 729.

6. Rousseau, *Émile*, 328.

7. The case is brilliantly made in Cordelia Fine, *Delusions of Gender* (London: Icon Books, 2010).

8. Vergil, *Aeneid*, 1.630.

9. Rousseau, *Émile*, 185.

10. Ibid., 187.

11. Smith, *Theory*, 1.3.1, 4; 44.

12. Aaron Ben-Ze'ev, "Envy and Inequality," *Journal of Philosophy* 89, no. 11 (Nov. 1992): 551–81.

13. W. Somerset Maugham, *Cakes and Ale* (New York: Vintage Books, 2000), 10.

14. Hesiod, quoted in Ben-Ze'ev, "Envy and Inequality," 556.

15. D. Kahneman and A. Tversky, "The Simulation Heuristic," in Kahneman, Slovic, and Tversky, *Judgment under Uncertainty: Heuristics and Biases* (New York: Cambridge University Press, 1982).

16. Spinoza, *Ethics*, part 5, note to prop. 39.

17. Ralph Gomory and Richard Sylla, "The American Corporation," *Daedalus* (Spring 2013): 109.

18. Ibid., 103.

19. Emmanuel Saez, "Striking it Richer: The Evolution of Top Incomes in the United States," http://elsa.berkeley.edu/~saez/saez-UStopincomes-2011.pdf.

20. These are quite typical figures for banking and credit card borrowing in the UK at present.

21. Quoted at http://highpaycommission.co.uk/submissions/what-the-highly-paid-think-of-high-pay/.

22. It is ironic in this connection that as Europe's prime lender, Germany has been adamant in exacting austerity and Draconian debt repayment schedules from the poorer countries of Europe, perhaps forgetting that it was the farsighted forgiveness of huge Nazi debts

by other countries that alone enabled its own postwar economic recovery.

23. Quoted in Norman Dixon, *The Psychology of Military Incompetence* (London: Cape, 1976), 374.

24. Hume, *Treatise*, 3.2.1, 481.

25. John Adams, "Defence of the Constitutions of Government of the United States of America," in *The Works of John Adams, Second President of the United States: With a Life of the Author, Notes and Illustrations, by his Grandson Charles Francis Adams* (Boston: Little, Brown and Co., 1856), 4:407.

CHAPTER 6
RESPECT

1. Kant, *Critique of Practical Reason*, 203, 5:162.

2. Immanuel Kant, *Groundwork of the Metaphysics of Morals*, ed. Mary Gregor (Cambridge: Cambridge University Press, 1998), 38, 4:429; hereafter *Groundwork*.

3. This is brought out in Langton's discussion of Maria von Herbert's case, described above.

4. Kant, *Groundwork*, 15, 4:402; 31, 4:421.

5. In *Plato's Republic* (London: Grove Atlantic, 2006), 32–33, I describe how exactly this reply is used by the Athenians, bent on enslaving or destroying the Melians, in a famous passage from Thucydides.

6. Kant, *The Metaphysics of Morals*, 186, 6:435; italics in original.

7. Ibid., 187, 6:436.

8. See William Ian Miller, *Losing It* (New Haven: Yale University Press, 2011).

9. Kant, *The Metaphysics of Morals*, 192, 6:443.

10. Although as we saw in the introduction, in other places he is a good deal more wary of inclinations and desires across the board.

11. Adam Smith is typically excellent on this; see *Theory*, 3.2.2, 5.

12. Aristotle, *Nicomachean Ethics*, 1123a–1125a. The quotations are from the translation by Terence Irwin (Indianapolis: Hackett Books, 1985).

13. Bertrand Russell, *History of Western Philosophy* (London: Allen & Unwin, 1961), 188.

14. It is quite unlikely that Newton was sincere, since by and large he was a rather unpleasant character.

15. Erasmus, *The Praise of Folly*, 34–35.

16. John Milton, "The Reason of Church-Government," in *The Works of John Milton* (New York: Columbia University Press, 1931–40), 3:260.

17. David Hume, *Dialogues Concerning Natural Religion*, ed. J.C.A. Gaskin (Oxford: Oxford University Press, 1993), part 5, 69.

18. See, for instance, Robert Johnson, *Self-improvement: An Essay in Kantian Ethics* (Oxford: Oxford University Press, 2011).

19. Kant, *Metaphysics of Morals*, 173, 6:418.

20. Lord Shaftesbury, *A Letter Concerning Enthusiasm*, in *Characteristicks of Men, Manners, Opinion, Times* (London, 1711), 1:11.

CHAPTER 7
TEMPTATION

1. Jean-Jacques Rousseau, *The Social Contract, and Discourses*, ed. G.D.H. Cole (London: Dent, 1973), 306.

2. David Hume, *Enquiry Concerning the Principles of Morals*, ed. T. Beauchamp (Oxford: Oxford University Press, 1998), section 9, part 1, 146–47.

3. Friedrich Nietzsche, *The Antichrist*, section 62.

4. In using the masculine singular pronoun for the Deity, I defer to a familiar usage; it should be apparent from the text that mentally I put it in inverted commas; indeed, it shortly becomes clear that any pronoun is inept. Meanwhile "He, it, she, or they" would be cumbersome.

5. Matthew 10:29.

6. This is the so-called apophatic tradition; its guiding thought is expressed in a nice simile I once read, that religions are like public swimming pools: most noise comes from the shallow end. I was amused recently to find that one proponent of the apophatic ideal, the writer Karen Armstrong, has authored some fifteen books explaining

how silence is the only adequate response to God. It has to be the right kind of silence, of course, not that of the sleeper, the inebriate, or the pothead.

7. Kant, *Groundwork*, 21, 4:408.

8. Émile Durkheim, *The Elementary Forms of Religious Life*, trans. Carol Cosman (Oxford: Oxford University Press, 2001), 46.

9. Quoted in Richard Fletcher, *Moorish Spain* (London: Phoenix, 1992), 106.

10. Spenser, *The Faerie Queene*, book 1, canto 4, lines 32–49.

11. The importance of reading Milton this way is the theme of Stanley Fish's seminal criticism, *Surprised by Sin: The Reader in "Paradise Lost"* (New York: Macmillan, 1967). In his preface, Fish announces that in the course of the poem "the reader is confronted with evidence of his corruption and becomes aware of his inability to respond adequately to spiritual conceptions."

12. Milton, *Paradise Lost*, 4.460–68.

13. Ibid., 4.807–9.

14. Ibid., 9.538–48.

15. *The Works of John Milton*, ed. F. A. Patterson et al. (New York: Columbia University Press, 1931–40), 15:87–89. Quoted in Fish, *Surprised by Sin*, 40.

16. The phrase comes from Allan Gibbard, *Wise Choices, Apt Feelings: A Theory of Normative Government* (Cambridge, MA: Harvard University Press, 1990). We consider the yoke of necessity more in chapter 8.

17. A. D. Nuttall, *The Alternative Trinity: Gnostic Heresy in Marlowe, Milton, and Blake* (Oxford: Oxford University Press, 1998).

18. For Augustine on the subject, see my *Lust* (Oxford: Oxford University Press, 2004), 57–63.

19. *Paradise Lost*, 9.692–94.

20. Ibid., 9.739–43.

21. Ibid., 9.780–81.

22. There is a philosophical moral here as well. The neurophysiologist Benjamin Libet and others following him have found that excitement in the motor cortex, anticipating action, can precede what the subject reports as the conscious moment of decision. Such results have been supposed to undermine any notion of free will, since the system is already primed and, as it were, lumbering down the runway before

the conscious moment of decision. But Milton and Sartre show us that this is wrong, since freedom is not to be thought of as a matter of some kind of intrusion from the executive mind into the (distinct!) brain at the exact moment of decision. It is the susceptibility to all the voices that precede the moment of decision and that set the way we look at the world as we decide. In 2003 the United States declared war on Iraq, and the fact that military and logistical preparations were in train days and weeks before it did so does not absolve it from the responsibility for doing so.

23. *Paradise Lost*, 9.786–90.

24. Ibid., 9.1008–11.

25. Hume, *Treatise*, 2.3.4, 421.

26. Ibid., 422.

CHAPTER 8
INTEGRITY, SINCERITY, AUTHENTICITY

1. Bernard Williams and J.J.C. Smart, *Utilitarianism, For and Against* (Cambridge: Cambridge University Press, 1973).

2. Elizabeth Ashford, "Utilitarianism, Integrity and Partiality," *Journal of Philosophy* 97 (2000): 421–39.

3. Bernard Knox, *The Heroic Temper: Studies in Sophoclean Drama* (Berkeley: University of California Press, 1964), 5.

4. The phrase comes from Aeschylus's play *Agamemnon*, line 217. Oddly enough, Matthew Arnold, the Victorian critic, thought that *Antigone* could not mean much for moderns because we no longer believe in the gods of the underworld. He failed to notice their symbolic role, figuring the stringency of the obligation Antigone carries. And Arnold's prophecy was dead wrong. In the twentieth century, the play became a major vehicle for exploring moral versus political obligation; Bertholt Brecht's timely version was played in 1948.

5. A. C. Bradley, *Shakespearean Tragedy: Lectures on Hamlet, Othello, King Lear, Macbeth*, 2nd ed. (London: Macmillan, 1905), 18.

6. Lionel Trilling, *Sincerity and Authenticity* (Cambridge, MA: Harvard University Press, 1972).

7. I owe the observation to Stefan Collini.

8. Christine Korsgaard has influentially promoted this view; see, for instance, *The Sources of Normativity* (Cambridge: Cambridge University Press, 1996). Hegel himself saw the Romantic ideal as just a step in the dialectical dance toward a more perfect, religious self-consciousness.

9. I have found it helpful to read the sections of Plato where he advocates banishing the artists as if his targets were something more like entertainment executives. Then many parents, virtually anyone of moderately refined taste, and anyone concerned about the world of the future, might sympathize with him. See my *Plato's Republic*, esp. chapter 15.

10. Jean-Paul Sartre, *Essays in Existentialism* (New York: Citadel Press, 1993), 160–64.

11. Robert Musil, *The Man without Qualities* (London: Martin, Secker & Warburg, 1961), 1:71.

CHAPTER 9
ENVOI

1. Quoted in Felix Martin, *Money: The Unauthorised Biography* (London: Bodley Head, 2013), 277. Martin's entire book is a fascinating exploration of the danger of misguided ideas about the nature of money and what it measures.

2. Thomas Traherne, *Centuries of Meditations* (London: Private publication, 1908). Reproduced at Christian Classics Ethereal Library, http://www.ccel.org/ccel/traherne/centuries.html, under "The First Century," paragraph 29. Philosophers and logicians may be suspicious of the contradiction of everyone being the sole heir of something, but the dissonance forces us to think harder about Traherne's vision. In this vision to embrace yourself, you must embrace the world. See also the comment on the last six lines of Sonnet 62 near the end of chapter 1.

Index